I0415712

August 2012

MILITARY DISABILITY SYSTEM

Improved Monitoring Needed to Better Track and Manage Performance

Accountability ★ Integrity ★ Reliability

MILITARY DISABILITY SYSTEM

Improved Monitoring Needed to Better Track and Manage Performance

GAO

Accountability * Integrity * Reliability

Highlights

Highlights of GAO-12-676, a report to congressional committees

Why GAO Did This Study

Since 2007, DOD and VA have jointly operated IDES—which is intended to expedite benefits for injured servicemembers. IDES replaced the departments' separate processes for evaluating servicemembers for fitness and disability. Initially a pilot at 3 military treatment facilities, IDES is now in place at military treatment facilities worldwide. In previous reports, GAO identified a number of challenges as IDES expanded to more facilities, including staffing shortages and difficultly meeting timeliness goals.

In light of IDES' expansion, GAO was asked to examine: (1) the extent to which DOD and VA are meeting IDES timeliness and servicemember satisfaction performance goals, and (2) steps the agencies are taking to improve IDES performance. GAO analyzed IDES timeliness and customer satisfaction data, visited six IDES sites with varying performance, and interviewed DOD and VA officials.

What GAO Recommends

To improve monitoring of IDES timeliness and satisfaction, GAO recommends that DOD and VA work together to (1) develop plans for completing the ongoing business process review and implementing any resulting recommendations and (2) improve the accuracy of case information at the point of data entry; and that (3) DOD consider alternative approaches to measuring satisfaction. DOD and VA concurred with GAO's recommendations.

View GAO-12-676. For more information, contact Daniel Bertoni at (202) 512-7215 or bertonid@gao.gov.

What GAO Found

Case processing times under the Integrated Disability Evaluation System (IDES) have increased over time, and measures of servicemember satisfaction have shortcomings. Since 2008, annual average processing times for IDES cases have steadily climbed, while the percentage of cases meeting established timeliness goals declined. Average case processing times reached 394 and 420 days for active and reserve component members in fiscal year 2011—compared to goals of 295 and 305 days, respectively, and just 19 percent of active duty and 18 percent of guard or reserve servicemembers completed the process and received benefits within established goals. Of the four phases comprising IDES, the medical evaluation board phase increasingly fell short of timeliness goals, while the physical evaluation board phase, although meeting goals, was taking increasingly more time to complete. With respect to servicemember satisfaction with the IDES process, GAO found shortcomings in how these data are collected and reported, such as unduly limiting who is eligible to receive a survey and computing average satisfaction scores in a manner that may overstate them. Department of Defense (DOD) officials told GAO they are considering alternatives for gauging satisfaction with the process.

Timeliness for IDES Cases Resulting in VA Benefits (by year case completed)

Source: GAO analysis of DOD and VA data

DOD and Veterans Affairs (VA) are taking steps to improve IDES performance, but progress to date is uneven and it is too early to assess their overall impact. For example, VA increased resources for completing exams and disability ratings while the Army is hiring additional staff for its medical evaluation boards. VA has met exam timeliness goals in the past several months, but other resources have yet to translate into lower processing times. DOD and VA are pursuing system upgrades so that staff and managers at IDES facilities can better track and manage the progress of servicemembers' cases. IDES officials have been working with the military services to correct case data that were inaccurately entered into VA's IDES tracking system, but have not yet identified a permanent solution to improve the accuracy of data input. Finally, DOD, with VA's assistance, is in the early stages of an in-depth review of the entire IDES process and its supporting IT systems. This effort is intended to improve understanding of how each step contributes to overall processing times and identify opportunities to streamline the process and supporting systems. However, timeframes for completing the review or issuing recommendations have yet to be established.

_____ United States Government Accountability Office

Contents

Figures

Abbreviations

DOD	Department of Defense
IDES	integrated disability evaluation system
MEB	medical evaluation board
PEB	physical evaluation board
VA	Department of Veterans Affairs
VTA	Veterans Tracking Application
WCP	Office of Warrior Care Policy
WWCTP	Office of Wounded Warrior Care & Transition Policy

United States Government Accountability Office
Washington, DC 20548

August 28, 2012

The Honorable Patty Murray
Chairman
The Honorable Richard Burr
Ranking Member
Committee on Veterans' Affairs
United States Senate

The Honorable Joseph I. Lieberman
Chairman
The Honorable Susan M. Collins
Ranking Member
Committee on Homeland Security and Governmental Affairs
United States Senate

Servicemembers who are injured in war or as the result of accidents and illnesses may face a difficult transition as they leave the military and become veterans. In response to concerns that wounded, ill, or injured servicemembers had to undergo two complex disability evaluations—first by the Department of Defense (DOD) then by the Department of Veterans Affairs (VA)—DOD and VA jointly designed a new integrated disability evaluation process to expedite the delivery of benefits to servicemembers. In November 2007, DOD and VA began pilot testing the integrated disability evaluation system (IDES) at three military treatment facilities in the Washington, D.C. area, and expanded the number of sites over time. As of October 1, 2011, IDES had replaced the military services' existing—or "legacy"—disability evaluation systems for almost all new disability cases.

Past GAO work highlighted challenges DOD and VA experienced while piloting the IDES and recommended a number of improvements. For instance, we reported in December 2010[1] that insufficient staff and logistical challenges contributed to delays in completing IDES cases and recommended the agencies take steps to ensure adequate staffing levels and develop a systematic process for monitoring caseloads. In response

---

[1] GAO, *Military and Veterans Disability System: Pilot Has Achieved Some Goals, but Further Planning and Monitoring Needed*, GAO-11-69 (Washington, D.C.: Dec. 6, 2010).

GAO-12-676 Military Disability Evaluation

to ongoing concerns with IDES performance, this report provides information on (1) the extent to which DOD and VA are meeting IDES performance goals, and (2) steps DOD and VA are taking to improve IDES performance.

In conducting our work, we obtained DOD timeliness and customer satisfaction data from the inception of IDES in 2007 to December 2011. We assessed the reliability of these data and analyzed them to look for changes in performance over time; factors that may help or hinder performance; and relationships between servicemember satisfaction and case outcomes and timeliness. We supplemented these analyses with site visits to six military treatment facilities, where we spoke with DOD and VA staff as well as some servicemembers involved in the IDES process.[2] We selected these facilities to obtain perspectives from sites in different military services and geographical regions and with varying caseloads and performance outcomes. For both research objectives, we interviewed key officials involved with IDES at DOD, VA, and each of the military services, and reviewed pertinent reports, guidance, plans, relevant federal laws, regulations, directives, and other documents. We conducted this performance audit from May 2011 to August 2012, in accordance with generally accepted government auditing standards. These standards require that we plan and perform the audit to obtain sufficient, appropriate evidence to provide a reasonable basis for our findings and conclusions based on our audit objectives. We believe the evidence obtained provides a reasonable basis for our findings and conclusions based on our audit objectives.

Background

The Disability Evaluation Process

The IDES process begins at a military treatment facility when a physician identifies one or more conditions that may interfere with a servicemember's ability to perform his or her duties.[3] The process

---

[2] We visited the facilities at Joint Base Andrews and Fort Meade, Maryland; Naval Hospital Bremerton and Joint Base Lewis-McChord (Madigan Army Medical Center), Washington; and Forts Hood and Sam Houston, Texas.

[3] A physician is required to identify a condition that may cause the member to fall below retention standards after the member has received the maximum benefit of medical care.

involves four main phases: the Medical Evaluation Board (MEB), the Physical Evaluation Board (PEB), transition out of military service (transition), and VA benefits.

MEB phase: In this phase, medical examinations are conducted and decisions are made by the MEB regarding a servicemember's ability to continue to serve in the military. This phase involves four stages: (1) the servicemember is counseled by a DOD board liaison on what to expect during the IDES process; (2) the servicemember is counseled by a VA case manager on what to expect during the IDES process and medical exams are scheduled;[4] (3) medical exams are conducted according to VA standards for exams for disability compensation by VA, DOD, or contractor physicians, and (4) exam results are used by the MEB to identify conditions that limit the servicemember's ability to serve in the military.[5] Also during this stage, a servicemember can seek a rebuttal, or an impartial medical review by a physician not on the MEB, or both.

PEB phase: In this subsequent phase, decisions are made about the servicemember's fitness for duty, disability rating and DOD and VA disability benefits, and the servicemember has opportunities to appeal those decisions. This includes: (1) the informal PEB stage, an administrative review of the case file by the relevant military branch's PEB without the presence of the servicemember; (2) VA rating stage, where a VA rating specialist prepares a rating that covers the conditions that DOD determined made a servicemember unfit for duty and any other conditions claimed by the servicemember to VA.[6] This rating is prepared for use by both agencies in determining disability benefits. In addition, servicemembers have several opportunities to appeal different aspects of their disability evaluations: a servicemember dissatisfied with the decision on whether he or she is fit for duty may request a hearing with a "formal" PEB; a servicemember who disagrees with the formal PEB fitness

---

[4] In this report, "DOD board liaisons" refers to DOD Physical Evaluation Board Liaison Officers, while "VA case managers" refers to VA Military Service Coordinators.

[5] This evaluation is based on the results of the medical exams, the member's medical records, and input from the member's commanding officer.

[6] VA determines the degree to which veterans are disabled in 10 percent increments on a scale of 0 to 100 percent. If VA finds that a veteran has one or more service-connected disabilities with a combined rating of at least 10 percent, the agency will pay monthly compensation.

decision can, under certain conditions, appeal to the reviewing authority of the PEB;[7] and a servicemember can ask for VA to reconsider its rating, but only for conditions found unfitting by the PEB.

Transition phase: If the servicemember is found unfit to serve, he or she enters the transition phase and begins the process of separating from the military. During this time, the servicemember may take accrued leave. Also, DOD board liaisons and VA case managers provide counseling on available benefits and services, such as job assistance.

VA benefits phase: A servicemember found unfit and separated from service becomes a veteran and enters the VA benefits phase. VA finalizes its disability rating after receiving evidence of the servicemember's separation from military service. VA then starts to award monthly disability compensation to the veteran.

DOD and VA established timeliness goals for the IDES process to provide VA benefits to active duty servicemembers within 295 days of being referred into the process, and to reserve component members within 305 days (see fig. 1). DOD and VA also established interim timeliness goals for each phase and stage of the IDES process. The overall timeframes are intended to represent an improvement over the legacy disability evaluation system, which was estimated to take 540 days to complete.

---

[7] The reviewing authorities of PEBs in the respective services are the Air Force Personnel Council, the Army Physical Disability Agency, and the Navy Council of Review Boards.

Figure 1: Steps of the IDES Process and Timeliness Goals

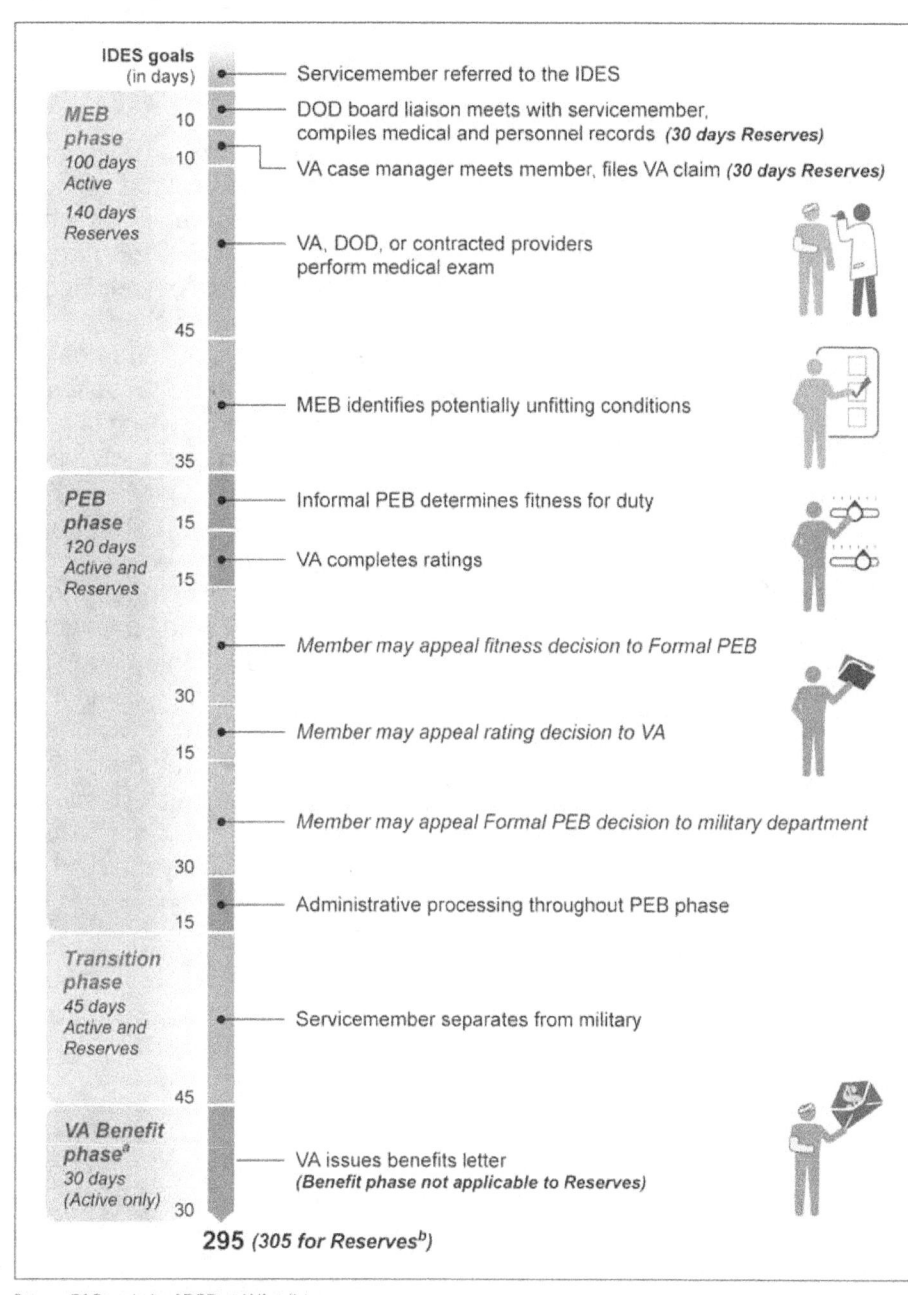

IDES goals (in days)	Step
	Servicemember referred to the IDES
MEB phase 100 days Active 140 days Reserves — 10	DOD board liaison meets with servicemember, compiles medical and personnel records *(30 days Reserves)*
10	VA case manager meets member, files VA claim *(30 days Reserves)*
45	VA, DOD, or contracted providers perform medical exam
35	MEB identifies potentially unfitting conditions
PEB phase 120 days Active and Reserves — 15	Informal PEB determines fitness for duty
15	VA completes ratings
30	*Member may appeal fitness decision to Formal PEB*
15	*Member may appeal rating decision to VA*
30	*Member may appeal Formal PEB decision to military department*
15	Administrative processing throughout PEB phase
Transition phase 45 days Active and Reserves — 45	Servicemember separates from military
VA Benefit phase[a] 30 days (Active only) — 30	VA issues benefits letter *(Benefit phase not applicable to Reserves)*

295 *(305 for Reserves[b])*

Source: GAO analysis of DOD and VA policies.

[a]Not all reservists complete the VA benefit phase and thus DOD does not apply the 30-day goal for this phase to reservists. For those reservists who do go through the VA benefits phase, this time is reflected in the overall time in IDES.

In addition to timeliness, the agencies also established a performance goal of having 80 percent of servicemembers satisfied with the IDES process. DOD measures satisfaction through surveys conducted after the completion of the MEB, PEB, and transition phases. Each survey consists of approximately 30 questions, including 4 questions that ask about the servicemember's satisfaction with the overall IDES process up to that point. Reported satisfaction rates for each phase are based on an average of responses to these four questions, and reported overall satisfaction with IDES (which is used to track the percent satisfied under the performance goal) is an average of satisfaction rates for the three phases.

Rollout of IDES and Enrollment

From the original 3 pilot military treatment facilities in the Washington, D.C., area,[8] the IDES has expanded to 139 military treatment facilities in the U.S. and several other countries. DOD and VA first added 24 military treatment facilities to the pilot in fiscal years 2009 and 2010, bringing the pilot total to 27. In 2010, DOD and VA leadership decided to implement the IDES world-wide, and did so in 4 stages between October 2010 and September 2011, adding 112 military treatment facilities. As IDES expanded, the number of new cases enrolled in IDES has also increased, totaling 18,651 in fiscal year 2011 (see fig. 2).

[8] The three original pilot sites were Walter Reed Army Medical Center, Washington, D.C.; National Naval Medical Center, Bethesda, Maryland; and Malcolm Grow Air Force Medical Center, Andrews Air Force Base.

GAO-12-676 Military Disability Evaluation

Figure 2: IDES Cases Enrolled and Completed by Fiscal Year

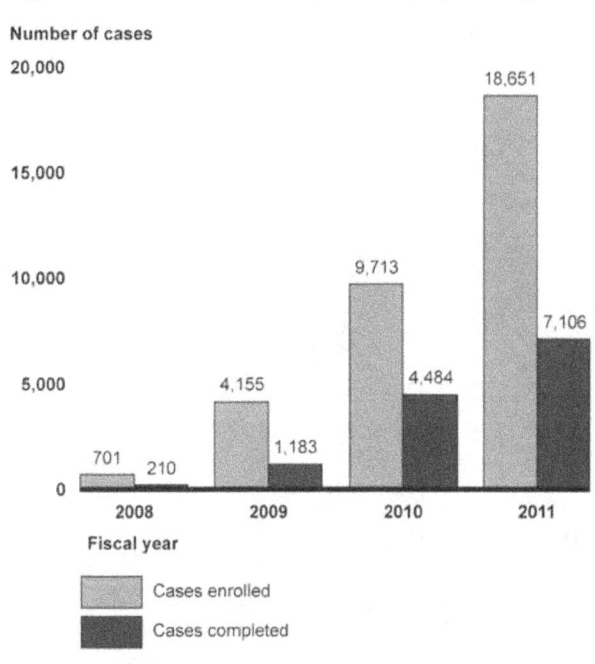

Source: GAO analysis of DOD and VA data.

Note: Cases completed include those who exited the IDES process, including those who received benefits or returned to duty.

IDES caseloads vary by service, but the Army manages the bulk of IDES cases. Of new cases referred to IDES in fiscal year 2011, about 64 percent were in the Army, and much of the growth in caseload has been in the Army. Additionally, active duty servicemembers make up the majority of IDES cases, with about 88 percent of new cases in fiscal year 2011 involving this group (see fig. 3).

GAO-12-676 Military Disability Evaluation

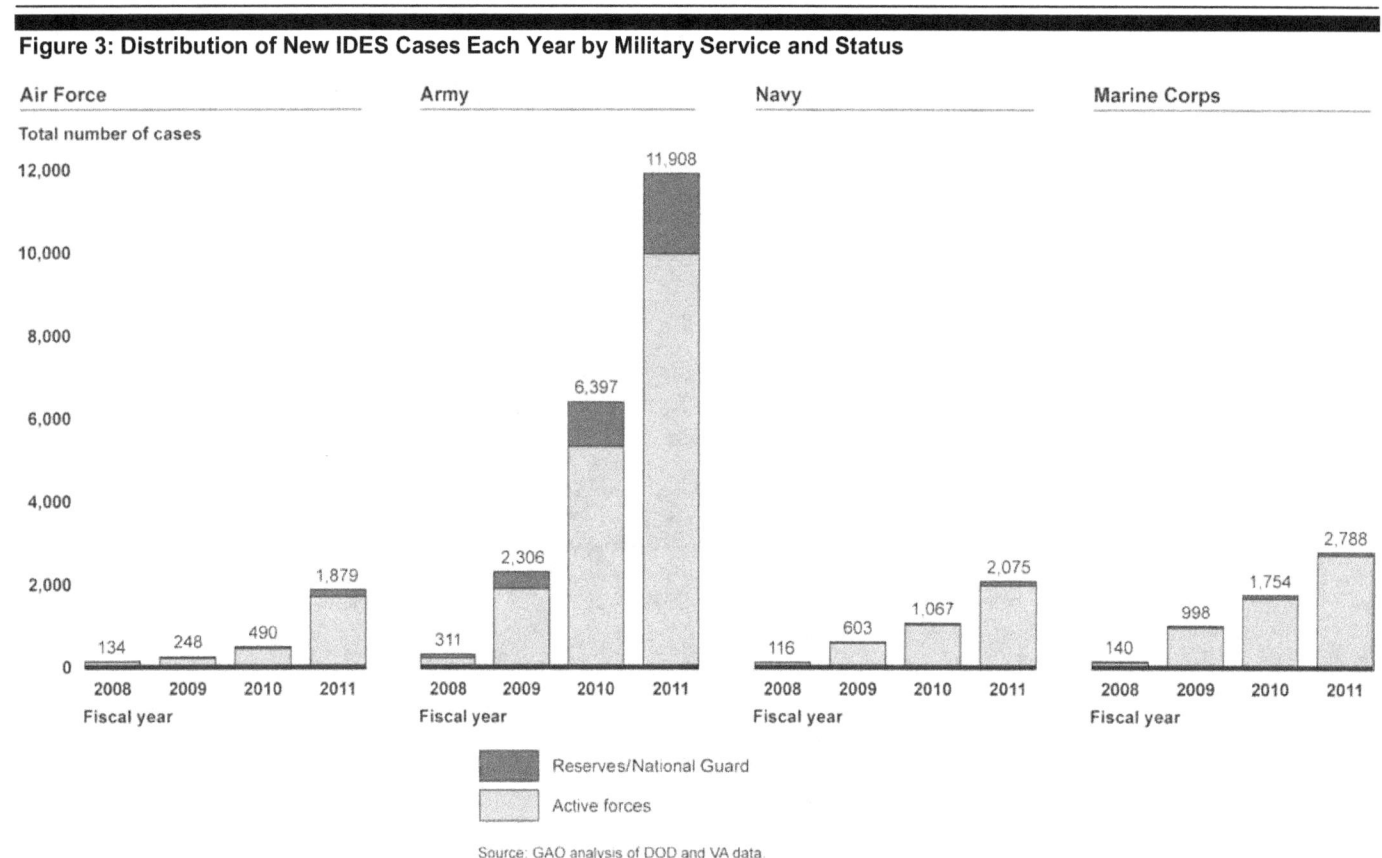

Figure 3: Distribution of New IDES Cases Each Year by Military Service and Status

Air Force | Army | Navy | Marine Corps

Total number of cases

Legend:
- Reserves/National Guard
- Active forces

Source: GAO analysis of DOD and VA data.

IDES Processing Times Increased Over Time, While Measures of Servicemember Satisfaction Have Shortcomings

Overall IDES Case Processing Times Steadily Increased Since the Start of IDES

IDES timeliness has worsened since the inception of the program. Since fiscal year 2008, the average number of days for servicemember cases to be processed and receive benefits increased from 283 to 394 for active duty cases (compared to the goal of 295 days) and from 297 to 420, for reserve component cases (compared to the goal of 305 days) (see fig. 4).[9]

Figure 4: Average Processing Times and Number of Completed Cases Resulting in Benefits by Fiscal Year of IDES Completion

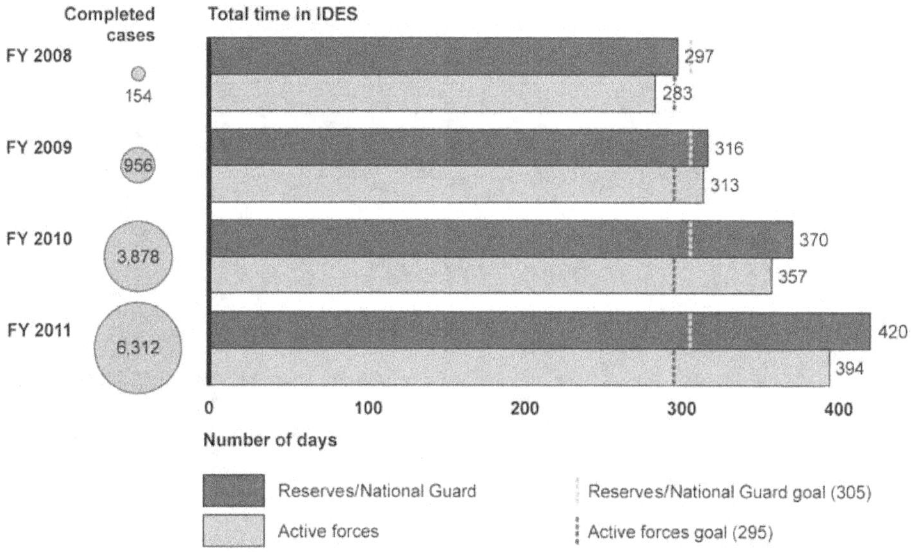

Source: GAO analysis of DOD and VA data.

Along with increasing average processing times, the percent of IDES cases awarded benefits within timeliness goals has steadily declined. DOD's and VA's current goal is to complete 60 percent of IDES cases on time. In fiscal year 2008, an average of 63 percent of cases for active duty servicemembers and 65 percent for reservists completed the process and received benefits within the timeliness goals; by fiscal year 2011 this was down to 19 and 18 percent respectively (see fig. 5). These trends also hold when considering all cases that completed the IDES process regardless of outcome, although overall processing times were shorter. (See app. III for more information on case processing times regardless of outcome.)

---

[9] When processing times are broken down by the year of completion, as in Figure 4, the average processing times in the first few years are lower since cases with longer processing times after the program's inception in fiscal year 2008 would not show up in the data until fiscal year 2009 or later.

Figure 5: Percentage of Cases Resulting in Benefits Meeting and Not Meeting Overall Processing Time Goals by Fiscal Year of IDES Completion

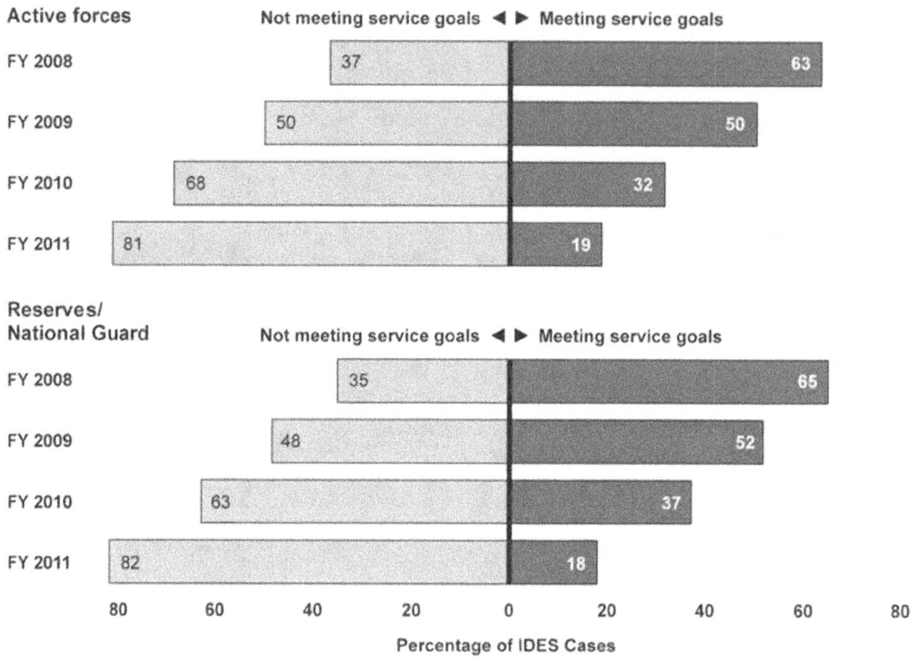

Active forces   Not meeting service goals ◄ ► Meeting service goals

FY 2008   37 | 63
FY 2009   50 | 50
FY 2010   68 | 32
FY 2011   81 | 19

Reserves/
National Guard   Not meeting service goals ◄ ► Meeting service goals

FY 2008   35 | 65
FY 2009   48 | 52
FY 2010   63 | 37
FY 2011   82 | 18

80   60   40   20   0   20   40   60   80

Percentage of IDES Cases

Source: GAO analysis of DOD and VA data.

Key Contributors to Timeliness Problems Include Lengthy Medical Evaluations and Servicemember Separation Activities

When examining timeliness across the four phases that make up IDES, data show that average processing time regularly fell short of goals for three—MEB, Transition, and VA Benefits. For example, for cases that completed the MEB phase in fiscal year 2011, active duty and reserve component members' cases took an average of 181 and 188 days respectively to be processed, compared to goals of 100 and 140 days. For the PEB phase, processing times increased over time, but were still within the established goal of 120 days. Along with increasing average processing times, the percentage of cases meeting goals for most phases has generally declined (see fig. 6). In particular, the MEB and Transition phases have lower percentages of cases meeting goals than the other phases in most years, especially for active duty cases.

GAO-12-676 Military Disability Evaluation

Figure 6: Percent of Cases Meeting Timeliness Goals for each Phase of IDES by Fiscal Year of Completion

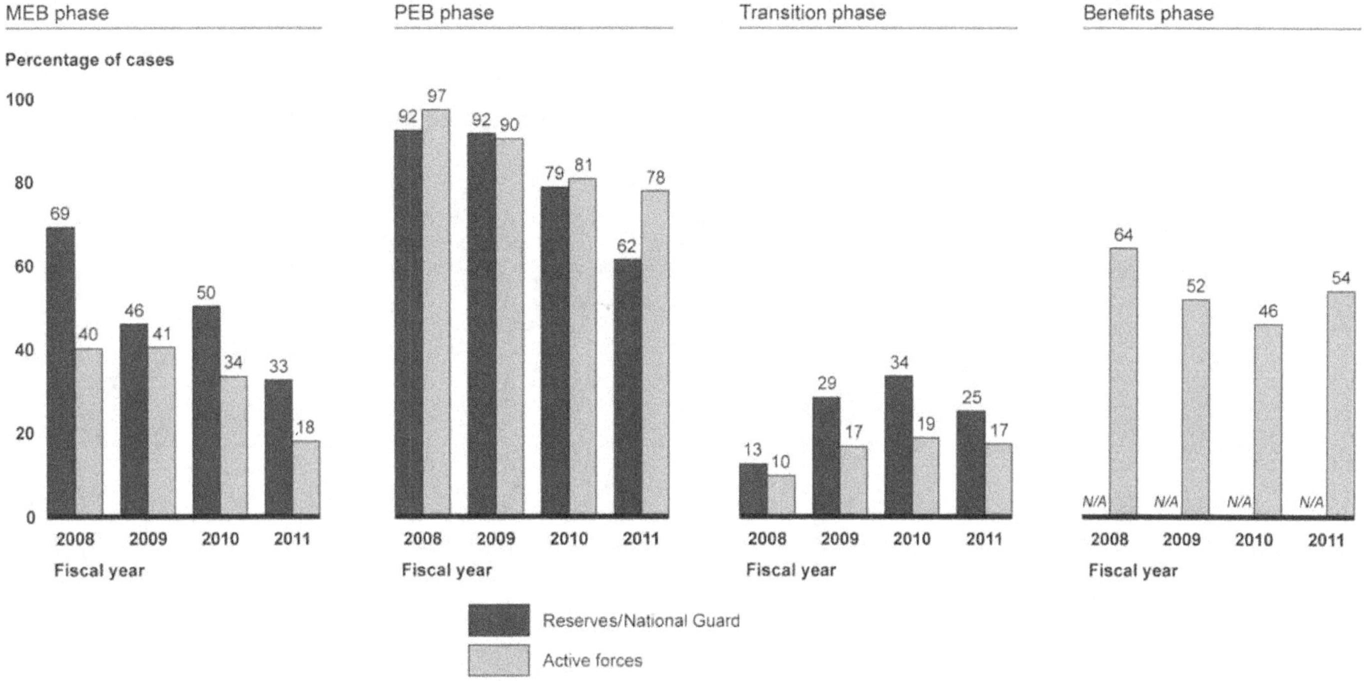

MEB phase | PEB phase | Transition phase | Benefits phase

Percentage of cases

Reserves/National Guard
Active forces

Source: GAO analysis of DOD and VA data.

MEB Phase

As noted above, the MEB phase was a key contributor to increases in overall processing times between 2008 and 2011 for both active duty servicemembers and reservists for cases that have completed the IDES process regardless of outcome (table 1).

Table 1: Average Processing Times for MEB Phase for Completed Cases by Fiscal Year of Completion (in days)

Component	Goal	FY 2008	FY2009	FY2010	FY2011
Active	100	114	126	141	181
Reserve	140	128	153	158	188

Source: GAO analysis of DOD and VA data.

To obtain a better understanding of more recent timeliness trends within the MEB phase, GAO analyzed MEB timeliness of all cases—all fiscal years combined—that completed the MEB process by sorting them into two groups: (1) those that completed the entire IDES process, and (2) those that had not yet completed IDES but completed the MEB phase. As shown in figure 7, for the group that completed IDES, 30 percent of active

GAO-12-676 Military Disability Evaluation

duty servicemembers and 18 percent of reservists missed the goal by more than 90 days. For those still in IDES, representing more recent data, the picture is slightly better for active duty servicemembers with 37 percent of cases meeting the MEB goal and 25 percent missing the goal by more than 90 days. However, the percentage of reserve component members who missed the goal by more than 90 days increased from 18 to 28 percent.

Figure 7: Percent of Cases Completing MEB Within or in Excess of Goals All Fiscal Years Combined

Completed MEB and IDES

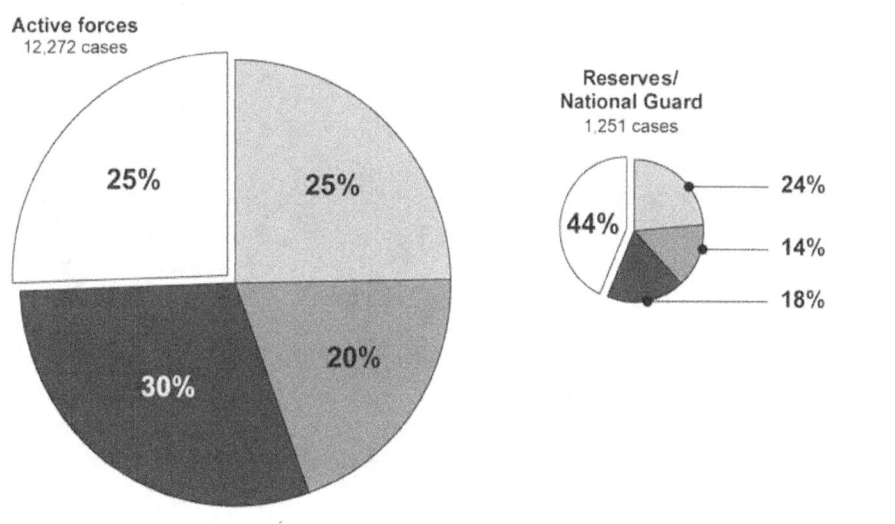

Completed MEB but are still enrolled in IDES

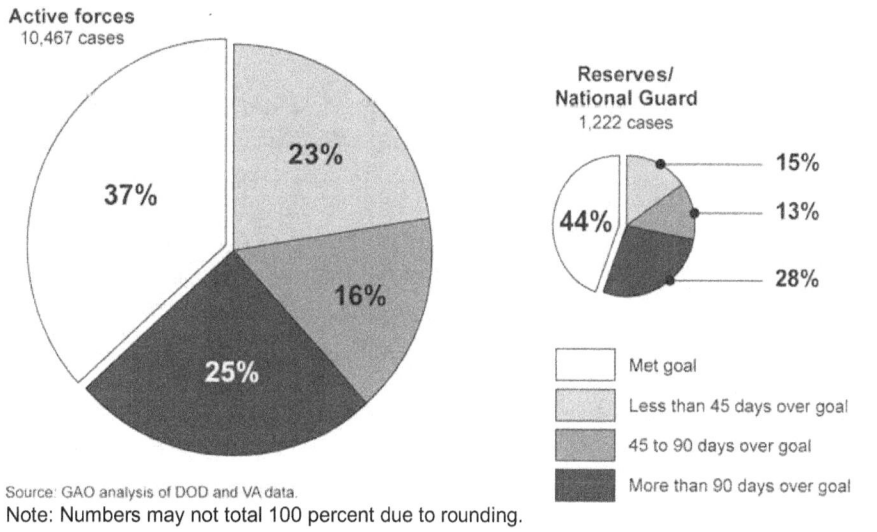

Source: GAO analysis of DOD and VA data.
Note: Numbers may not total 100 percent due to rounding.

For those servicemembers who were still enrolled in the MEB phase as of December 2011, the data show that 41 percent of active duty and 33 percent of reserve component servicemember cases had already missed the goal processing times (see fig. 8). Of these, 15 percent of active duty and 10 percent of reservist component servicemember cases missed the goal by more than 90 days.[10]

Figure 8: Timeliness of Cases Enrolled in MEB Stage as of December 2011

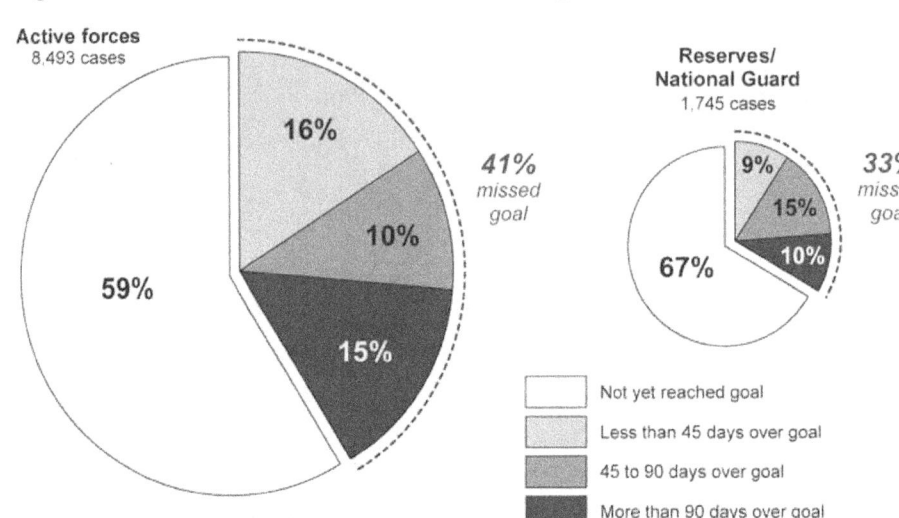

Active forces
8,493 cases

16%

10%

59%

15%

41%
missed goal

Reserves/
National Guard
1,745 cases

9%

15%

10%

67%

33%
missed goal

☐ Not yet reached goal

☐ Less than 45 days over goal

☐ 45 to 90 days over goal

■ More than 90 days over goal

Source: GAO analysis of DOD and VA data.
Note: Numbers may not match numbers in the body of this report or total 100 percent due to rounding.

Within the MEB phase, significant delays have occurred in completing medical examinations (medical exam stage) and delivering an MEB decision (the MEB stage). For cases completing the MEB phase in fiscal year 2011, 31 percent of active duty and 29 percent of reservist cases met the 45-day goal for the medical exam stage and 20 percent of active duty and 17 percent of reservist cases met the 35-day goal for the MEB stage. Officials at some sites we visited told us that MEB phase goals were difficult to meet and not realistic given current resources. For example:

- Some military officials noted that they did not have sufficient numbers of doctors to write the narrative summaries of exam results needed to

---

[10] Our data were for cases in the MEB phase as of December 31, 2011. For cases that had not yet been in the MEB for 100 days (the MEB goal), we cannot predict whether they will be timely cases or not. For instance some of these cases entered the MEB phase just days before the cutoff date GAO chose.

GAO-12-676 Military Disability Evaluation

complete the MEB stage in a timely manner.[11] One facility noted that while they have 7 doctors, they would need 11 additional doctors and 10 technician assistants to process cases through the initial medical exam and other additional disability specific examinations in a timely manner. Further, officials at another Army base we visited noted that there was a shortage of doctors and DOD board liaisons and that they had difficulty recruiting such staff due to the remote location of the base.

- At all the facilities we visited, officials told us DOD board liaisons and VA case managers had large case loads. While DOD has established a goal of 1 board liaison for every 20 servicemembers,[12] the ratios varied widely by military treatment facility with a range from 1:1 as the lowest to the highest of 1:75 according to recent data. Because of high case loads and a reported increase in the complexity of cases, staff at one facility reported a liaison to servicemember ratio of 1:80 and noted that liaisons must often prioritize cases to deal with the most pressing issues first. As a result, cases that might otherwise be quick to process take longer simply because they are waiting to be processed. Liaisons are often working overtime and weekends to keep up with cases.

Monthly data produced by DOD subsequent to the data we analyzed show significantly improved timeliness for the medical exam stage (66 percent of active duty cases met the goal in June 2012) and some improvement for the MEB stage (40 percent of active duty cases met the goal in the month of June 2012). However, it is too early to tell whether these improvements will continue going forward. (See app. III for DOD reported monthly data, October 2011 – June 2012[13].)

PEB Phase

Since fiscal year 2008, the majority of cases have completed the PEB phase under the goal of 120 days, however, PEB timeliness has still worsened over time. In 2011, 78 percent of active duty and 62 percent of reservist cases that completed the entire IDES process met the PEB goal.

---

[11] As previously noted, the narrative summary documents the medical conditions and the impact of these conditions on the servicemembers' ability to perform their military duties.

[12] VA's goal is 1 case manager for every 30 new cases.

[13] DOD did not provide monthly data on the percentage of reservist cases meeting these stage goals. See app. III for more information on monthly processing times.

The average processing time was 93 days for active duty servicemembers and 116 for reservists (see table 2).

Table 2: Average Processing Time in PEB Phase of IDES for Completed Cases (in days)

Component	Goal	FY 2008	FY2009	FY2010	FY2011
Active	120	42	58	80	93
Reserve	120	41	60	83	116

Source: GAO analysis of DOD and VA data.

Despite meeting the overall PEB goal in fiscal year 2011, established goals were not met for any of the interim PEB stages, including the informal PEB and VA rating stages which are the two stages all servicemembers must complete. For all cases that completed the PEB phase in fiscal year 2011, only 38 percent of active duty and 38 percent of reservists' cases received an informal PEB decision within the 15 days allotted. Further, only 32 percent of active duty and 27 percent of reservist cases received a preliminary VA rating within the 15-day goal. (see table 3).

Table 3: Average Processing Time for PEB Stages of IDES for Completed Cases (in days)

Stage of PEB Phase	Component	Goal	FY 2008	FY2009	FY2010	FY2011
Informal Physical Evaluation Board (IPEB)	Active	15	17	12	21	26
	Reserve	15	15	12	19	29
VA preliminary rating	Active	15	6	20	27	33
	Reserve	15	7	26	32	43
VA rating reconsideration[a]	Active	15	3	11	14	32
	Reserve	15	8	29	18	30
Formal Physical Evaluation Board (FPEB)[a]	Active	30	13	39	63	81
	Reserve	30	33	38	55	69
FPEB appeal[a]	Active	30	196	5	100	103
	Reserve	30	20	23	13	169

Source: GAO analysis of DOD and VA data

[a]These stages are appeals. Fewer servicemembers completed each of the appeal stages compared to the non-appeal stages, but the average days spent within the appeal stages generally and significantly surpassed the goal times.

Regarding delays with the VA rating, VA officials told us that staffing has been a challenge at their IDES rating sites and that this has slowed case processing. Monthly data produced by DOD subsequent to the data we analyzed show similar trends for the informal PEB and VA preliminary rating stages. As of June 2012 (most recent data available), active duty cases showed slight improvements in timeliness for the informal PEB stage (41 percent of cases meeting the goal and processing times averaging 24 days). The VA rating stage, on the other hand, showed slight declines in timeliness (31 percent of cases meeting the established goal and processing times of 35 days) relative to FY 2011 averages for active duty servicemembers. However, as noted before, it is too early to tell the extent to which such trends will continue. (See app. III for DOD reported monthly data, October – June 2012.)

Also during this phase, IDES planners allocated the majority of overall PEB processing time (75 out of the 120 days) for appeals—including a formal PEB hearing and a reconsideration of the VA ratings. According to officials, while the three appeal stages do not happen for every case, appeals can significantly increase processing times for any one case. However, only 20 percent of cases completed in fiscal year 2011 actually had any appeals; calling into question DOD and VA's assumption on the prevalence and average effect of appeals, and potentially masking processing delays in other mandatory parts of the PEB phase.

Transition Phase

The transition phase has consistently taken longer than its 45-day goal—almost twice as long on average. While processing times improved slightly for cases that completed this phase in fiscal year 2011 (from 79 days in fiscal year 2010 to 76 days in fiscal year 2011 for active duty cases), timeliness has remained consistently problematic since fiscal year 2008 (see table 4).

Table 4: Average Processing Time in Transition Phase of IDES for Completed Cases (in days)

Component	Goal	FY 2008	FY2009	FY2010	FY2011
Active	45	88	80	79	76
Reserve	45	81	73	82	75

Source: GAO analysis of DOD and VA data.

DOD lacks comprehensive data on how servicemembers spend their time in the transition phase, which includes many different activities related to separation from the military. These activities vary widely depending on the case.[14] For example, during this phase servicemembers receive

---

[14] According to VA officials, reservists who are not on active duty do not have a transition phase.

mandatory training such as job training through the Transition Assistance Program and may also receive counseling such as pre-discharge Vocational Rehabilitation and Employment counseling. In addition, servicemembers may be placed on temporary duty while house hunting, or to allow for a servicemember's children to complete the school year before moving. Servicemembers may also take earned leave time—to which they are entitled—before separating from the service. For example, an Army official said that Army policy allows servicemembers to take up to 90 days of earned leave prior to separating, and that average leave time was about 80 days. Because many of these activities can occur simultaneously or in small intermittent segments of time, DOD officials said it is difficult to track which activities servicemembers participate in or determine how much time each activity takes. DOD is exploring options for better tracking how time is spent in this phase. Because a potentially substantial amount of the time in this phase may be for the personal benefit of servicemembers, DOD recently began reporting time in IDES with and without the transition phase included.

Benefits Phase

Processing time improved somewhat for the benefits phase (48 days in fiscal year 2010 to 38 days in fiscal year 2011), but continued to exceed the 30-day goal for active duty servicemembers (see table 5).[15]

Table 5: Average Processing Time in Benefits Phase of IDES for Completed Cases (in days)

Component	Goal	FY 2008	FY2009	FY2010	FY2011
Active	30	29	43	48	38

Source: GAO analysis of DOD and VA data.

Several factors may contribute to delays in this final phase. VA officials told us that cases cannot be closed without the proper discharge forms and that sometimes they do not receive this information in a timely manner from the military services. Additionally, if data are missing from the IDES tracking system (e.g., the servicemember already separated, but this was not recorded in the database), processing time will continue

---

[15] DOD and VA did not set a goal for reserve component servicemembers. As noted above, for purposes of this report, we opted to not include reserve component time spent in the VA benefit phase in our calculations phase because this goal applies to some but not all reservists, depending on their active duty status. Any time spent within the VA benefit phase is reflected within the overall processing time calculations for such reserve component servicemembers.

to accrue for cases that remain open in the system. Officials could not provide data on the extent to which these factors had an impact on processing times for pending cases, but said that once errors are detected and addressed, reported processing times are also corrected.

Shortcomings in the Design and Administration of Servicemember Surveys Hamper their Usefulness

In addition to timeliness, DOD and VA evaluate IDES performance using the results of servicemember satisfaction surveys. In principle, all members have an opportunity to complete satisfaction surveys at the end of the MEB, PEB, and transition phases; however, under current survey procedures servicemembers become ineligible to complete a survey for either the PEB or transition phases if they did not complete a survey in an earlier phase. Additionally, servicemembers who start but do not complete a phase are not surveyed. As such, DOD may be missing opportunities to obtain input from servicemembers who did not complete a prior survey or exited IDES in the middle of a phase.[16] Further, response rates may be affected because DOD does not survey servicemembers once they separate from the service and become veterans. While it is not necessary for DOD to survey all servicemembers at the end of every phase,[17] the percentage and characteristics of servicemembers covered by the survey (i.e., who completed a phase and were ultimately interviewed) may be insufficient to establish that the survey results are representative of servicemember satisfaction, especially for later phases. (See table 6 for response and coverage rates.) DOD officials recently told us that they will consider alternative survey eligibility requirements, including working with the Office of Management and Budget for permission to interview veterans. (For additional information regarding the timing of the survey, see app. II).

---

[16] DOD officials also told us that a servicemember may be surveyed simultaneously for a prior phase along with the phase just completed (e.g. the MEB and PEB phases). However, in some cases a significant amount of time may have passed since the servicemember completed the prior phase and, thus, it may be more difficult for the servicemember to isolate his or her satisfaction with a particular phase.

[17] DOD could interview a probability sample of servicemembers to accurately assess satisfaction with IDES in the population as a whole. A sample could decrease the cost of obtaining this information, because DOD would need to contact fewer servicemembers and the cost of surveys generally increases with the number of people interviewed. If properly designed and executed, a probability sample would provide estimates that would be equally valid as interviewing all servicemembers.

Table 6: Survey Response and Coverage Rates

Phase	Servicemembers who completed phase (N)	Servicemembers eligible to be surveyed (i.e., completed both phase and survey for prior phase, if applicable)	Servicemembers who completed survey	Response rate (Servicemembers who completed survey / Servicemembers eligible)	Coverage rate (Servicemembers who completed survey / Servicemembers who completed phase)
MEB	25,212	all	9,604	38.1%	38.1%
PEB	18,296	8,968	4,795	53.5%	26.2%
Transition	12,352	3,996	2,893	72.4%	23.4%

Source: GAO analysis of DOD and VA data.

In addition, alternate survey measures show lower satisfaction rates than those reported by DOD. Using DOD's measure, we found an overall satisfaction rate of about 67 percent since the inception of IDES. DOD defines a servicemember as satisfied if the average of his or her responses across several surveys is above 3 on a 5-point scale, with 3 denoting neither satisfied nor dissatisfied. However, using our alternate measure that defines servicemembers as satisfied only when all of their responses are 4 or above,[18] we calculated the satisfaction rate to be about 24 percent (see fig. 9).

---

[18] Using DOD's satisfaction measure, we found less than expected variation in satisfaction over time and across key case characteristics, such as component, military branch, final rating and final disposition. To better understand factors that may drive servicemember satisfaction, we included neutral responses in the category of "not satisfied" rather than counting such responses as "satisfied" in the manner that DOD did thus arriving at a measure that more strongly reflects satisfaction and might be a more sensitive indicator of factors affecting satisfaction for performance management purposes.

Figure 9: Comparison of Percent of Servicemembers Satisfied Using GAO and DOD Calculations for Overall Satisfaction

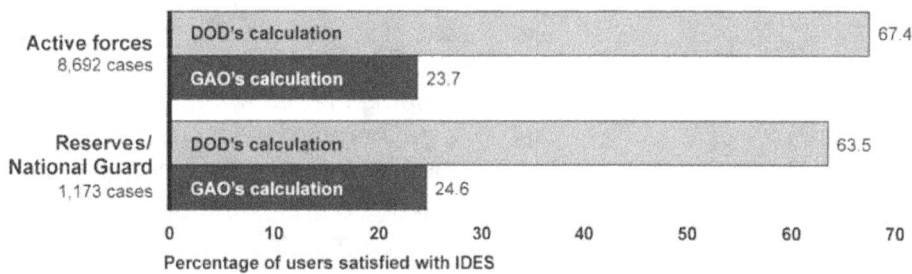

Source: GAO analysis of DOD and VA data.

Note: GAO combined reserve and national guard, while DOD reported satisfaction scores for guard and reserve separately.

Our calculation is a more conservative measure of satisfaction, because it rules out the possibility that a servicemember is deemed "satisfied" even when he or she is dissatisfied on one or more questions in the scale. While not incorrect, DOD's scale can mask pockets of servicemember dissatisfaction. For example, an individual may indicate that he or she is very dissatisfied with one phase of the program, but satisfied with other phases, and the overall satisfaction score can be the same as one for a servicemember who is generally satisfied across all phases of the process. Measuring satisfaction, or even dissatisfaction, in different ways may provide a more complete picture of satisfaction and how it varies in different circumstances, and thus may reveal areas where DOD could focus on improving management and performance.

Finally, using either DOD's or our calculated measure, we found that overall satisfaction did not vary much according to differences in the experiences of servicemembers. For example, our model estimated that satisfaction varied by no more than approximately five percentage points across branch, component, disenrollment outcome, sex, MEB exam provider, enlisted and officer personnel classes, and the number of claimed and referred conditions. While lack of variation could be a positive outcome signaling consistent treatment, it could equally mean that the survey does not measure opinions in enough detail to discriminate among servicemembers' experiences. Either way, such results provide little insight into identifying areas for improvement or effective practices. Further, while we found some association between servicemembers satisfaction and the timeliness of their case processing, we also found many servicemembers were highly dissatisfied even when their cases were completed on time, and many were highly satisfied even when their cases were not. For example, 68 percent of those who said that PEB timeliness was "very poor" completed the phase on time, and 55 percent of those who said that MEB timeliness was "very good" did not complete on time. The lack of variation and/or correlation between satisfaction and experiences of servicemembers—coupled with low coverage rates—raise questions about the value of the survey results as a performance measure and program evaluation tool. (See app. II for more information on servicemember satisfaction results.)

DOD is reconsidering its options for measuring customer satisfaction, but has yet to select a particular approach. As noted above, possible changes might include widening the criteria for who is eligible for the survey, modifying survey questions, changing when and how the survey is delivered, and changing how satisfaction is calculated. Officials already concluded that the survey, in its current form, is not a useful management tool for determining what changes are needed in IDES and said that it is expensive to administer—costing approximately $4.3 million in total since the start of the IDES pilot. Navy officials told us they believed that the satisfaction surveys could be made more useful if they knew whether servicemember's satisfaction was actually influenced by the servicemember's desired or actual outcome of the IDES process. Further, Army officials already determined that the DOD survey is of limited value, and are proceeding with plans to field their own survey in the hopes of obtaining more detailed information at the facility level. Because of fiscal constraints, DOD suspended the survey in December 2011, but officials told us that they hope to resume collecting data in fiscal year 2013.

We identified two potential alternatives to assessing servicemember experiences.

- *Surveying a sample of servicemembers*: While a census gives each servicemember a chance to describe his or her experiences with IDES, DOD could collect the same data at a lower cost by surveying a probability sample of servicemembers. If appropriately designed and executed, a sample would accurately represent all groups of servicemembers and produce the necessary data for important subgroups, such as facilities or branches. Since the cost of administering a survey is strongly related to the number of people surveyed, probability sampling could also allow DOD to assess servicemember experiences while substantially reducing data collection costs.

- *Exit interviews*: In-depth interviews with servicemembers, completed at disenrollment from IDES, could also yield more detailed and actionable information about the program. Although the current survey includes open-ended questions, it is primarily designed to collect standardized, quantitative measures of satisfaction with broad aspects of IDES, such as fairness and the performance of DOD board liaisons and VA case managers. As a result, the survey provides a limited amount of detailed feedback on particular facilities, staff members, and stages of the process that managers might use to improve the servicemember experience, decrease processing times, or reduce cost. In contrast, semi-structured exit interviews would allow servicemembers to provide this type of qualitative, detailed feedback. Interviewing servicemembers at the end of the process would also allow servicemembers to assess their overall experiences with IDES rather than at an earlier stage, without having completed the entire process. Exit interviews could also reach servicemembers who exit IDES without completing the process such as those who are returned to duty. Exit interviews, however, have the potential to be labor intensive and expensive.

Recent Actions and Ongoing Initiatives May Improve IDES Performance, but It Is Too Early to Assess Their Overall Impact

DOD and VA Took Steps to Address Previously Identified IDES Challenges

DOD and VA have undertaken a number of actions to address IDES challenges—many of which we identified in our past work. Some actions—such as increased oversight and staffing—represent important steps in the right direction, but progress is uneven in some areas.

Increased monitoring and oversight: We identified the need for agency leadership to provide continuous oversight of IDES in 2008[19] and the need for system-wide monitoring mechanisms in 2010. Since then, agency leadership has established mechanisms to improve communication, monitoring, and accountability.

- The secretaries of DOD and VA have met several times since February 2011 to discuss progress in improving IDES timeliness and have tasked their agencies to find ways to streamline the process so that the timeliness goals can be shortened. The secretaries also tasked their agencies to expand the use of expedited disability evaluations for severely combat-wounded servicemembers;[20] and develop a system to electronically transfer case files between DOD and VA locations.

- Senior Army and Navy officials regularly hold conferences to assess performance and address performance issues, including at specific facilities. With respect to the Army, meetings are led by the Army's vice-chief of staff and VA's chief of staff, and include reviews of performance where regional and local facility commanders provide feedback on best practices and challenges. For example, recent Army-VA conferences focused on delays in completion of preliminary ratings for Army PEBs by VA's Seattle rating site, efforts by the Army to increase MEB staffing, development of Army-wide IDES standardization guidance, and Army-VA electronic records interchange. Periodic meetings are also held between senior Navy medical and VA officials to discuss performance issues at Navy military treatment facilities.

VA holds its own biweekly conferences with local staff responsible for VA's portion of the process. These conferences are supplemented by a bi-weekly IDES "dashboard" that tracks performance data for portions of

---

[19] *Military Disability System: Increased Supports for Servicemembers and Better Pilot Planning Could Improve the Disability Evaluation Process*, GAO-08-1137 (Washington, D.C.: Sept. 24, 2008).

[20] In January 2012, senior agency officials decided to merge the DOD-VA Senior Oversight Committee into the DOD-VA Joint Executive Council, co-chaired by the Under Secretary of Defense (Personnel and Readiness) and the Deputy Secretary of Veterans Affairs. DOD and VA plan to establish a joint IDES working group under the Joint Executive Council. Meanwhile, the IDES has been incorporated into the agencies' Joint Strategic Plan, and agency stakeholders meet weekly to discuss IDES issues.

the IDES for which VA is responsible. According to VA officials, in addition to identifying best practices, these conferences focus on sites with performance problems and identify potential corrective actions. For example, officials said a recent conference addressed delays at Fort Benning, Georgia, and discussed how they could be reduced. VA officials noted that examiner staff were reassigned to this site and worked on weekends to address the problems at this site. In addition, senior VA health care officials hold periodic conferences with officials responsible for exams at IDES sites, to monitor performance.

Ensuring sufficient medical exam resources: In our December 2010 report, we noted that VA struggled to provide enough medical examiners (both VA employees and contractors) to meet demand and deliver exam summaries within its 45-day goal. For example, significant deficiencies in examiner staffing (particularly for mental health exams) at Fort Carson contributed to exams for active duty members taking an average of 140 days. To improve exam timeliness, VA hired more examiners and is devoting more resources at those sites where VA clinicians perform IDES exams. In addition, in July 2011, VA awarded a revised compensation and pension (including IDES) contract that provides more flexibility for VA to have contractors perform IDES exams at sites needing additional resources. As a result, VA can use contractors to conduct exams for regional offices beyond the 10 offices for which the contractor normally provides services. Also, VA contracted with 5 companies to provide short-term exam assistance at IDES sites needing it. Further, VA procedures allow reserve component servicemembers in remote locations to receive exams close to their homes. VA exam timeliness has improved and the agency met its 45-day goal for active component members in every month from August 2011 through June 2012. VA officials attributed improved exam timeliness, in part, to additional exam resources provided to IDES sites. (See app. III for additional information on fiscal year 2012 timeliness.)

Ensuring sufficient exam summaries: In our December 2010 report, we noted that some cases were delayed because VA medical exam summaries were not complete and clear enough for use in making rating and fitness decisions and needed to be sent back to examiners for additional work. VA officials told us that they have been reinforcing the importance of training and communication between rating staff and medical examiners as ways to improve exam summary sufficiency. For example, VA identified types of information which, if missing from an exam summary, would cause it to be insufficient, and has been training examiners to include such information. Additionally, VA noted that VTA now has the ability to track cases with insufficient exams by allowing staff to annotate information on exam summaries. However, staff are not required to provide this information and rules and procedures for its use have not been established.

Ensuring sufficient MEB staffing: In our December 2010 report, we noted that some sites had insufficient MEB physicians, leading to delays in completing the MEB phase. At that time, most of the 27 pilot sites were not meeting the 35-day goal, with average times for active component cases as high as 109 days. Meanwhile, DOD did not have sufficient board liaison staff to handle IDES caseloads. The Army is in the midst of a major hiring initiative intended to more than double staffing for its MEBs over its October 2011 level, which will include additional board liaison and MEB physician positions.[21] The Army reported having 610 full-time equivalent MEB staff positions in October 2011, and planned to hire up to 1,410; this would include 172 MEB physician and 513 board liaison positions. The Army also planned to hire an average of one contact representative per board liaison; these staff members assist the board liaisons with clerical functions, freeing more of the liaisons' time for counseling servicemembers. As of June 2012, the Army had filled 1,219 (86 percent) of the planned 1,410 positions.

Ensuring sufficient VA rating staff: In our December 2010 report, we noted that VA had insufficient staff at one of its rating sites to handle the demand for preliminary ratings, rating reconsiderations, and final VA benefit decisions. VA officials said that the agency has more than tripled the staffing at its IDES rating sites–from 78 to 262 positions. Further, VA has moved staff resources to IDES rating sites from other VA regional offices to provide short-term help in working down rating backlogs. Recent monthly data show an increase in the number of preliminary VA ratings completed, and a slight improvement in processing times. However, as noted before, it is too early to tell the extent to which such trends will continue. (See app. III for additional information on fiscal year 2012 timeliness.)

Improving completeness of reserve component members' records: Service officials noted that incomplete medical records and administrative

---

[21] The Army has physicians dedicated to MEB cases. In contrast, Navy and Air Force MEB determinations are prepared by physicians who perform other responsibilities, such as clinical treatment and supervision.

documentation, especially for reserve component members, often contribute to delays in the early IDES stages, including the VA exam stage. For example, a reserve unit may not have complete medical records for a member who received care from a private provider. When the servicemember enters the IDES, a board liaison is responsible for obtaining the private provider records before handing off the case to VA for exams. To address issues with reserve component servicemembers' records, the Army established an interim office in Pinellas Park, Florida in January 2011. For reserve component servicemembers who may require IDES referral, this office is tasked with obtaining records from the member's reserve unit; reviewing them to identify missing information; and, if necessary, requiring the reserve unit to obtain additional records to complete the case file. Staff at this office also determine whether the member needs IDES referral.[22] Army officials indicated that this office is expected to help reduce the backlog of Army reserve component cases in the IDES. However, Army officials noted that they are providing training to reserve units to improve their ability to maintain complete records on their servicemembers and eventually, the Army may discontinue this office if no longer needed.

Improving MEB documentation and decisions: In response to delays in completing the MEB stage, the Navy and Army have initiatives underway to help ensure the timely completion of narrative summaries and MEB decisions. For example, the Navy piloted electronic narrative summary preparation at Naval Hospital Camp Lejeune, North Carolina. In May 2012, after determining that the piloted process led to improved MEB completion timeliness, the Navy deployed electronic narrative summary preparation Navy-wide. In March 2011, the Army also deployed an abbreviated MEB narrative summary format, intended to provide better information for MEB and PEB decision making while helping reduce delays in the completion of these summaries by MEB clinicians. Incorporating feedback from its MEBs and PEBs, the Army expects the revised IDES template to reduce redundant information, make summaries simpler and easier to use, and standardize summary preparation across their sites.

---

[22] Originally, reserve component members determined to require IDES referral were referred to the MEB at Fort Gordon, Georgia. According to Army officials, these members are referred to one of 10 Army MEBs.

Resolving diagnostic differences: In our December 2010 report, we identified differences in diagnoses between DOD physicians and VA examiners, especially regarding mental health conditions, as a potential source of delay in IDES. We also noted inconsistencies among services in providing guidance and a lack of a tracking mechanism for determining the extent of diagnostic differences. In response to our recommendation, DOD commissioned a study on the subject. The resulting report confirmed the lack of data on the extent and nature of such differences, and noted that the Army has established guidance more comprehensive than the guidance DOD was developing. It also recommended that DOD or the other services develop similar guidance. A DOD official told us that consistent guidance across the services, similar to the Army's, was included in DOD's December 2011 IDES manual. Also, in response to our recommendation, VA took steps to modify the VTA database used to track IDES to collect information on diagnostic differences. The VTA upgrade was completed in June 2012 after several delays. The report also recommended that DOD and VA establish a committee to improve the accuracy of posttraumatic stress disorder ratings. DOD noted that training on diagnostic differences has been incorporated into its continuing medical education curriculum for military clinicians, but DOD considers the issue of posttraumatic stress disorder ratings largely resolved. Meanwhile, the Army's new IDES narrative summary template includes a section where the MEB clinician identifies any inconsistencies in the case record, including any diagnostic differences with VA examiners.

DOD and VA Are Addressing Shortcomings in Information Systems, but Efforts to Date Are Limited

DOD and VA are working to remedy shortcomings in information systems that support the IDES process. These shortcomings include VTA's lack of capability for local sites to track cases, and the potential for erroneous and missing data in VTA, affecting timeliness measurement. However, some efforts related to information systems are causing work inefficiencies, are still in progress, or otherwise are limited.

Improving local IDES reporting capability: DOD and VA are implementing solutions to improve the ability of local military treatment facilities to track their IDES cases, but multiple initiatives may result in redundant work efforts. Officials told us that the VTA—which is the primary means of tracking the completion of IDES cases—has limited reporting capabilities and staff at local facilities are unable to use it for monitoring the cases for which they are responsible. DOD and VA developed VTA improvements that will allow DOD board liaisons and VA case managers— and their supervisors—to track the status of their cases. VA included these operational reporting improvements in its June 2012 VTA upgrade. In the meantime, staff at many IDES sites have been using their own local systems to track cases and alleviate limitations in VTA. Further, the military services have been moving ahead with their own solutions. For instance, the Army has deployed its own information system for MEBs and PEBs Army-wide. In addition, DOD has also been piloting its own tracking system at 9 IDES sites.[23] As a result, staff at IDES sites we visited reported having to enter the same data into multiple systems. For example, board liaisons at Army MEBs Fort Meade and Joint Base Lewis-McChord reported entering data into VTA and the Army's new system, while board liaisons at Andrews Air Force Base reported entering data into VTA and DOD's pilot data system.

Improving IDES data quality: DOD is taking steps to improve the quality of data in VTA. Our analysis of VTA data identified erroneous or missing dates in at least 4 percent of the cases reviewed. Officials told us that VTA lacks adequate controls to prevent erroneous data entry, and that incorrect dates may be entered, or dates may not be entered at all, which can result in inaccurate timeliness data. For example, Army officials noted that some cases shown in VTA as very old were actually closed, but were missing key dates. In September 2011, DOD began a focused effort with the services to correct erroneous and missing case data in VTA. Officials noted that the Air Force and Navy completed substantial efforts to correct the issues identified at that time, but Army efforts continue. DOD and Army officials noted that additional staff resources are being devoted to cleaning up Army VTA data. While improved local tracking and reporting capabilities will help facilities identify and correct erroneous data, keeping VTA data accurate will be an ongoing challenge due to a lack of data entry controls. While DOD is currently assisting the services, DOD officials said they expect that eventually the services will be responsible for identifying and fixing data errors.

DOD and VA are also pursuing options to allow them to save time by replacing the shipping of paper case files among facilities with electronic file transfers. Requirements for an electronic case file transfer solution have been completed and DOD and VA officials expect to begin piloting it in August 2012. As a short-term solution, the Army and VA began using

---

[23] A DOD official told us that based on recent negative feedback, including from site visits, DOD is considering cancelling this pilot project.

an Army file transfer Web site to move IDES records between the Army's PEBs and the Seattle VA rating site in March 2012.[24] According to VA officials, this could save several days currently spent shipping paper files between these offices. VA officials noted that the same Web site is being used for transfers between the Navy PEB and Providence rating site. Meanwhile, the secretaries of Defense and Veterans Affairs tasked their staffs to develop standards for electronic IDES case files by July 2012.

DOD and VA are Pursuing Broader Solutions to Improving IDES Performance

Based on concerns of the Secretaries of DOD and VA about IDES delays, the departments have undertaken additional initiatives to achieve time savings for servicemembers. For example, in response to the secretaries' February 2011 directive to streamline the process, DOD and VA officials proposed a remodeled IDES process. In December 2011, senior agency leadership decided to postpone the pilot of a remodeled IDES process, and instead tasked the agencies to explore other ways to streamline the process.[25] As a result, DOD, with VA's assistance, began a business process review to better understand how IDES is operating and identify best practices for possible implementation. This review incorporates several efforts, including visits to 8 IDES sites to examine how the process was operating and identify best practices.[26] This review also includes the following:

- *Process simulation model*: Using data from site visits and VTA, DOD is developing a simulation model of the IDES process. According to a DOD official, this process model will allow the agencies to assess the impact of potential situations or changes on IDES processing times, such as surges in workloads or changes in staffing.

---

[24] As of March 2012, the Seattle rating site is responsible for cases from all 3 Army PEBs.

[25] Under this proposed process, VA would not begin work on a case until a servicemember was found to be unfit for military service by an informal PEB. The pilot was postponed in response to concerns raised by the military services and VA about specific changes to the existing process. For example, VA officials expressed concerns that the preliminary VA rating could occur long after the servicemember was found to be unfit for duty, which could cause the servicemember to seek a formal PEB hearing.

[26] In January and February 2012, teams visited Little Rock Air Force Base, Arkansas; Naval Medical Center San Diego, California; Fort Carson, Colorado; Wright-Patterson Air Force Base, Ohio; and Naval Medical Center Portsmouth, Virginia. In March 2012, a team visited Joint Base Andrews, Maryland, and Fort Eustis and Naval Health Clinic Quantico, Virginia, to examine the piloting of a new DOD-wide IDES information system.

- *Fusion diagram*: DOD is developing this diagram to identify the various sources of IDES data—including VA claim forms and narrative summaries—and different information technology systems that play a role in supporting the IDES process. Officials said this diagram would allow them to better understand and identify overlaps and gaps in data systems.

Ultimately, according to DOD officials, this business process review could lead to short- and long-term recommendations to improve IDES performance, potentially including changes to the different steps in the IDES process, performance goals, and staffing levels; and possibly the procurement of a new information system to support process improvements. However, a DOD official noted that these efforts are in their early stages, and thus there is no timetable yet for completing the review or providing recommendations to senior DOD and VA leadership. DOD officials indicated that they expect this to be a continuous IDES improvement process, including further site visits.

Finally, DOD is also developing guidance to expand implementation of an expedited disability evaluation process for servicemembers with catastrophic, combat-related conditions by allowing it to be operated at more military treatment facilities. DOD created this expedited process in January 2009 for servicemembers who suffer catastrophic, combat-related disabilities. Under an agreement with VA, the services can rate such members as 100 percent disabled without the need to use VA's rating schedule. However, according to DOD officials, the services report that no eligible servicemembers are using this process. Instead, servicemembers are having their cases expedited through the IDES informally. The revisions to DOD's policy would allow the expedited process to be used at additional military treatment facilities beyond the original 4 facilities.[27] According to DOD officials, this guidance will be part of a rewrite of DOD's key guidance documents, and was undergoing review at the time of our review.

Conclusions

By merging two duplicative disability evaluation systems, IDES shows promise for expediting the delivery of DOD and VA benefits to injured

---

[27] The original facilities were Walter Reed Army Medical Center, National Naval Medical Center, Brooke Army Medical Center (Fort Sam Houston), and Naval Medical Center San Diego.

servicemembers and is considered by many to be an improvement over the legacy process it replaced. However, nearly 5 years after its inception as a pilot, delays continue to affect the system and the contribution of various, complex factors to timeliness is not fully understood. Recent efforts by DOD and VA to better understand how different IDES processes contribute to timeliness are promising and may provide the departments with an opportunity to reassess resource levels and timeframes, and to make adjustments if needed. This information will also help to ensure that DOD and VA are making the best use of limited resources to improve IDES performance. However, it is not clear when these efforts will be complete or if any recommended actions will be implemented. DOD has also begun rethinking its approach to determining servicemember satisfaction with IDES. Our analysis of customer satisfaction data suggests that there are opportunities for improving the representativeness of the survey information collected and reconsidering the cost-effectiveness of the current lengthy surveys. Finally, providing local facilities the capability to track and generate reports on the status of their cases is long overdue and may empower local staff to better address challenges. However, tracking reports are only as good as the data that are entered into VTA, and DOD and VA can ensure the quality of these data through continuous monitoring. Meanwhile, the DOD-led business process review should identify and ultimately eliminate any redundant or inefficient information systems for tracking cases as well as for other IDES purposes.

Recommendations for Executive Action

1) To ensure that servicemember cases are processed and are awarded benefits in a timely manner, we recommend that the Secretaries of Defense and Veterans Affairs work together to develop timeframes for completing the IDES business process review and implementing any resulting recommendations.

2) To improve DOD's ability to measure servicemembers' satisfaction with the IDES process, we recommend that the Secretary of Defense develop alternative approaches for collecting more meaningful and representative information in a cost effective manner.

3) To ensure that IDES management decisions continue to be based upon reliable and accurate data, we recommend that the Secretaries of Defense and Veterans Affairs work together to develop a strategy to continuously monitor and remedy issues with VTA timeliness information. This could include issuing guidance to facilities or developing best practices on preventing and correcting data entry errors; and developing

reporting capabilities in VTA to alert facilities to potential issues with their data.

Agency Comments and Our Evaluation

We provided a draft of this report to DOD and VA for review and comment. In their written comments, which are reproduced in appendixes IV and V, DOD and VA both concurred with our recommendations. VA also provided technical comments, which we incorporated as appropriate.

While concurring with our recommendations, DOD also commented that our discussion of IDES surveys contained inaccuracies, but did not specify the inaccurate information in our draft report. In a subsequent communication, DOD officials noted that our draft inaccurately described DOD's decision to not survey veterans. We corrected this information accordingly. Further, while VA concurred with our recommendation that it work with DOD to develop timeframes for completing the IDES business process review and implementing any resulting recommendations, VA stated that DOD is leading the business process review, and therefore should develop the timeframes for completing the review. We have revised this report to clarify that DOD is leading the business process review, but we did not alter the recommendation because we believe that it is important for VA to work closely with DOD, including in developing review timeframes.

As agreed with your offices, unless you publicly announce the contents of this report earlier, we plan no further distribution until 30 days from the report date. At that time, we will send copies of this report to the appropriate congressional committees, the Secretary of Defense, the Secretary of Veterans Affairs, and other interested parties. The report is also available at no charge on the GAO Web site at www.gao.gov.

If you or your staff members have any questions about this report, please contact me at (202) 512-7215 or at bertonid@gao.gov. Contact points for our Offices of Congressional Relations and Public Affairs may be found on the last page of this report. Staff members who made key contributions to this report are listed in appendix VI.

Daniel Bertoni
Director, Education, Workforce,
and Income Security Issues

Appendix I: Objectives, Scope, and Methodology

In conducting our review of the Integrated Disability Evaluation System (IDES), our objectives were to examine (1) the extent to which the Departments of Defense (DOD) and Veterans Affairs (VA) are meeting IDES performance goals, and (2) steps DOD and VA are taking to improve IDES performance. We conducted this performance audit from May 2011 to August 2012, in accordance with generally accepted government auditing standards. These standards require that we plan and perform the audit to obtain sufficient, appropriate evidence to provide a reasonable basis for our findings and conclusions based on our audit objectives. We believe the evidence obtained provides a reasonable basis for our findings and conclusions based on our audit objectives.

Review of IDES Timeliness Data

To determine the extent to which IDES is meeting established timeliness goals, we analyzed data collected through VA's Veterans Tracking Application (VTA) database. While VA manages VTA, both DOD and VA staff enter data into VTA, and the evaluation of IDES data is primarily conducted by staff at DOD's Office of Warrior Care Policy (WCP).[1] WCP provided us with a dataset that was current as of January 1, 2012 and contained data spanning back to the inception of IDES in late 2007. This data export included data on a total of 39,260 cases. Of these cases, 34,185 were active duty servicemembers and 5,068 were Reserve/Guard servicemembers.[2] This VTA data set contained demographic data for each individual IDES case as well as a record of dates for when servicemembers reached various milestones in IDES.[3] Overall and interim IDES timeliness calculations are based on computing the number of days elapsed between appropriate milestone dates. For example, overall timeliness for servicemembers that receive benefits is calculated as the number of days between the individual being referred into the IDES and the date on which his or her VA benefits letter is issued. We met with staff at WCP to ensure we used appropriate variables when calculating timeliness. We also met with officials at VA to discuss the calculations used to determine the timeliness of cases.

---

[1] DOD's Office of Warrior Care Policy changed its name from the Office of Wounded Warrior Care and Transition Policy (WWCTP) in 2012.

[2] The number of active and Reserve components cases do not add up to the number of total cases because seven cases did not have a component code in the data.

[3] Demographic data included such information as gender, personnel class, service branch, component, and the number of conditions claimed and referred.

We took a number of steps to assess the reliability of VTA data and ultimately found the data to be sufficiently reliable for the purposes of our audit. Past GAO work[4] relied on VTA data, and therefore we took a number of steps to follow up on past assessments of VTA.

- We interviewed DOD and VA and determined that internal controls on VTA data had not changed substantially since our past review.

- We conducted electronic testing of the VTA data and generally found low rates of missing data or erroneous dates pertinent to our analysis—approximately 4 percent of cases.[5] For IDES cases in which we found missing dates or dates out of sequence, we excluded those cases from all of our analyses. While there were some instances in which the erroneous dates may be justified, we excluded the entire case from our analysis if any such dates appeared at any point in the VTA database. Such data included cases in which (1) there was no MEB referral date signifying the start of IDES process, and (2) the ending date preceded the beginning date of the IDES phase (resulting in timeliness calculations appearing as a negative amount of time).

- We also conducted a limited trace-to-file process to determine whether date fields in VTA were an accurate reflection of the information in IDES case files. Specifically, we compared VTA dates in 15 IDES cases completed in fiscal year 2011 against the dates in the corresponding paper files. In comparing dates, we allowed for a discrepancy of 5 days in dates to allow for the possibility that dates may have been entered into the database after an event took place. Ninety-three percent of the dates we traced back to the original file documents were found to be accurate, that is falling within our 5 day allowance.

---

[4] GAO, *Military and Veterans Disability System: Pilot Has Achieved Some Goals, but Further Planning and Monitoring Needed*, GAO-11-69 (Washington, D.C.: Dec. 6, 2010).

[5] Our analysis found an additional 11 percent of cases with dates missing for stages in the IDES program—dates that were not critical to our analyses. We believe that many if not most of these cases of missing data might be explainable. Servicemembers do not always pass through every step of the process and we believe this may explain some portion of missing dates. However, without looking at case files for all of these cases or the VTA data in more detail we cannot determine what portion of those 11 percent have a reasonable explanation for being missing.

Analysis Conducted Using VTA Data

For the cases meeting our criteria for reliability, we analyzed timeliness data for those cases that had completed the entire IDES process or had completed each of the four IDES phases. We specifically:

- Identified the total number of cases enrolled each fiscal year[6] from FY 2008 through 2011, by active as well as National Guard and reserve servicemembers, and by military branch of service.[7]

- Identified the number of cases that completed the entire IDES process for each fiscal year from fiscal year 2008 through fiscal year 2011. We analyzed completed cases in two different ways: (1) those who completed the process and received VA benefits and (2) those who completed the IDES with any outcome (such as permanent retirement, Temporary Disability Retirement List, return to duty, etc.). In order to be able to make comparisons across cases with different outcomes for a given point in time, we defined fiscal year by using the VTA variable "final disposition date". We did this because most completed cases—regardless of outcome—have a final disposition date in VTA. In contrast to our approach, VA use the "VA benefit date" variable to determine fiscal year of completion for cases resulting in benefits. As such, their number of cases and timeliness calculations by fiscal year differed from ours, although overall trends are similar.

- Identified the number of cases that completed each phase of IDES and the interim stages within each phase, again by fiscal year (fiscal years 2008 through 2011).

- Computed timeliness statistics for the completion of the IDES process, phases, and stages against the performance goals set by DOD and VA, such as average days and percent meeting goals.
- Computed number and percent of cases where a servicemember appealed a decision made during the IDES process, by fiscal year.

---

[6] We did not review the data on a monthly basis because this is done in DOD's monthly reports and we wanted to provide a longer term perspective of the evolution of the IDES program.

[7] While we have data through December for fiscal year 2012, we did not include these data in our analysis because we sought to compare completed fiscal years.

For the purposes of this report, GAO opted to not include reserve
component time spent in the VA benefit phase in our calculations for
overall time because the 30 days allotted for this phase is not included in
the 305-day overall goal for the reserve component.

GAO also performed analyses similar to those above, except that we
grouped cases according to the year in which they were enrolled in IDES.
(See app. II for more detail on these analyses.) Additionally, we analyzed
timeliness for cases that had not yet completed the MEB stage as of the
date we received the VTA data.

Review of IDES Customer Satisfaction Data

To determine the extent to which IDES is meeting its customer
satisfaction goals, we analyzed data collected from IDES customer
satisfaction surveys conducted at the end of three phases: MEB, PEB
and Transition. These surveys are administered by telephone by
contractors hired by DOD. The dataset we received contained survey
responses for individual servicemembers from the beginning of the IDES
pilot to December 2011, at which time administration of the survey was
suspended. Additionally, we matched individual survey responses with
information from VTA to gain additional understanding into how customer
satisfaction varied according to different factors such as timeliness and
case outcome. We matched survey and VTA data using the unique case
identifier attached to each IDES case, maintaining the anonymity of the
servicemembers. See appendix II for the results of additional analyses we
conducted using survey data and survey data matched with VTA data.

In the course of our review we concluded that the survey data were
sufficiently reliable for our purposes. We interviewed relevant officials at
DOD and their contractors about eligibility requirements and the
administration of the surveys. Further, we met with DOD and their
contractors on multiple occasions to discuss the calculations used to
determine response rates for the survey and servicemembers' level of
satisfaction. See appendix II for more details on GAO's review of
response rates.

Identifying Challenges and Actions Taken to Improve Performance

To identify challenges in implementing IDES as well as steps taken to
improve performance, we visited six military treatment facilities. During
the site visits, we interviewed officials involved in implementing IDES from
both DOD and VA, including military facility commanders and
administrators, DOD board liaisons, military physicians involved in MEB
determinations, DOD legal staff, VA case workers, VA or contract

examiners, and administrators at VA medical clinics and regional offices.
Additionally, we interviewed servicemembers who were currently enrolled
in the IDES process. We selected the six facilities to obtain perspectives
from sites in different military services, geographic areas, and their ability
to meet timeliness goals for different phases of the process (see table 7).
In addition, we visited the Air Force's Formal Physical Evaluation Board at
Randolph Air Force Base, Texas. During this visit we observed a hearing
and met with board members to obtain a better understanding of the
process.

Table 7: Selected Characteristics of IDES Pilot Sites Visited as of May 2011

Military treatment facility	Military service	State	IDES caseload	Average exam times (goal = 45 days)	Average MEB stage times (goal = 35 days)	Average Total IDES time (goal = 295 days)
Joint Base Andrews	Air Force	Maryland	511	24	56	472
Fort Hood	Army	Texas	1,976	31	107	334
Joint Base Lewis-McChord	Army	Washington	1,069	46	102	339
Fort Meade	Army	Maryland	543	35	140	556
Fort Sam Houston	Army	Texas	1,336	65	72	412
Naval Hospital Bremerton	Navy	Washington	199	52	14	348

Source: GAO analysis of DOD's June 2011 DES Monthly Report.

Note: Processing times listed in table are for active duty cases.

We also interviewed officials in various offices at DOD and VA involved in
implementing IDES. At DOD, these offices included Warrior Care Policy;
Office of the Assistant Secretary of Defense (Reserve Affairs); Office of
the Deputy Chief Management Officer; Air Force Physical Disability
Division; Army Physical Disability Agency; Navy Physical Evaluation
Board; Air Force Surgeon General; Army Medical Command; and Navy
Bureau of Medicine and Surgery. At VA, we interviewed officials in the
Veterans Benefits Administration, Veterans Health Administration, and
the VA/DOD Collaboration Service. Furthermore, we reviewed relevant
documents, including DOD and VA policies, federal laws, regulations,
directives[8] and guidance, a study produced for DOD on diagnostic
variances, and plans to streamline IDES or improve performance.

---

[8] Including Directive-Type Memorandum 11-015, which establishes policies, assigns
responsibilities, and prescribes procedures for the IDES.

Appendix II: Additional Timeliness and Satisfaction Analyses

This appendix provides additional information on the timeliness of the IDES process and servicemember satisfaction with it. First, we use timeliness data to examine whether changes over time in processing times and the percentage of cases meeting timeliness goals look any different when cases are grouped according to the fiscal year in which the cases were first enrolled rather than the fiscal year in which the cases were completed.[1] Second, we use survey data to examine different measurements of servicemember satisfaction with IDES, how satisfaction varied according to various servicemember characteristics, response and coverage rates for the servicemembers surveyed, and how the survey respondents differed from nonrespondents.[2]

With respect to timeliness, we find generally similar trends for cases grouped by fiscal year of enrollment versus fiscal year of completion, with some key differences. Organizing cases by completion date results in shorter average processing times in 2008, since only those cases that are processed quickly could be completed in the first year of IDES. As such, organizing cases by enrollment date provides a better estimate of the processing times for the early IDES cases. However, this approach results in shorter processing times in 2011, the most recent full year of the program, since only cases that finish quickly can be analyzed.

With respect to satisfaction, we find that the particular index used to summarize servicemembers' responses can affect the proportion reported as being "satisfied" or "dissatisfied" with IDES overall. DOD's index suggests that 67 percent of servicemembers have been satisfied since the IDES program began, but a reasonable alternative measure we developed suggests that only 24 percent of servicemembers have been satisfied. Using this measure, satisfaction varies only slightly across many important groups of servicemembers, such as by disenrollment outcome,

---

[1] We consider processing times overall, for the four phases of IDES (MEB, PEB, Transition, and VA Benefits), Active Duty, Reserve, or National Guard status, and for servicemembers receiving benefits versus all servicemembers regardless of the outcome of their cases.

[2] Response rates refer to the percentages of servicemen who responded to the surveys among those who DOD deemed eligible. For the MEB survey, eligibles included all servicemen who completed the MEB phase, but for the PEB and Transition surveys eligibles included only those who completed those phases and also completed the prior surveys. Coverage rates refer the percentages of servicemen that responded to each survey among those who completed each phase, regardless of whether they completed prior surveys.

suggesting that available program data cannot precisely explain satisfaction outcomes. Also, servicemembers surveyed may not represent the servicemembers who completed the different phases of IDES well enough to generalize to them, given the low response rates to the MEB survey and fact that being selected for latter (PEB and Transition) surveys were conditional on completing the MEB survey.

Overall IDES Timeliness: Processing Times and Percent of Cases Meeting Timeliness Goals

Average IDES processing times for completed cases resulting in benefits generally worsened since 2008, especially for active duty cases, regardless of whether cases are grouped by the fiscal year in which they were completed (fig. 10) or by the fiscal year in which they were enrolled (fig. 11). The notable exception is when fiscal year 2011 is the year of enrollment. However, caution must be used when examining cases enrolled in 2011 because over 15,600 service members of the 18,651 (or at least 84 percent) who entered IDES in fiscal year 2011 did not have an outcome in 2011 and were enrolled in IDES as of January 1, 2012,[3] potentially changing the distribution of processing times as they proceed through IDES.

---

[3] GAO's latest data export from the VTA database included data through January 1, 2012.

**Figure 10: Average IDES Processing Times by Year of Completion, for Completed
Cases Resulting in Benefits**

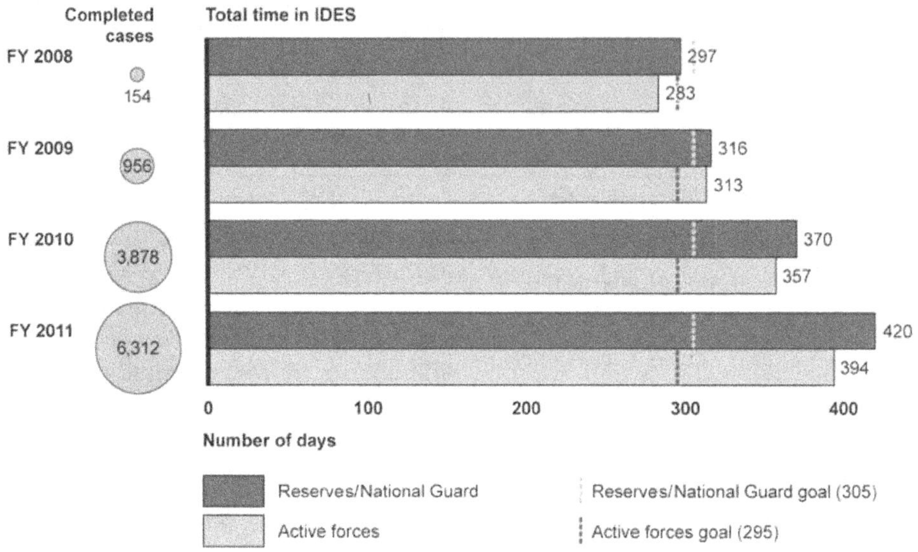

Source: GAO analysis of DOD and VA data.

**Figure 11: Average IDES Processing Times by Fiscal Year of Enrollment for
Completed Cases Resulting in Benefits**

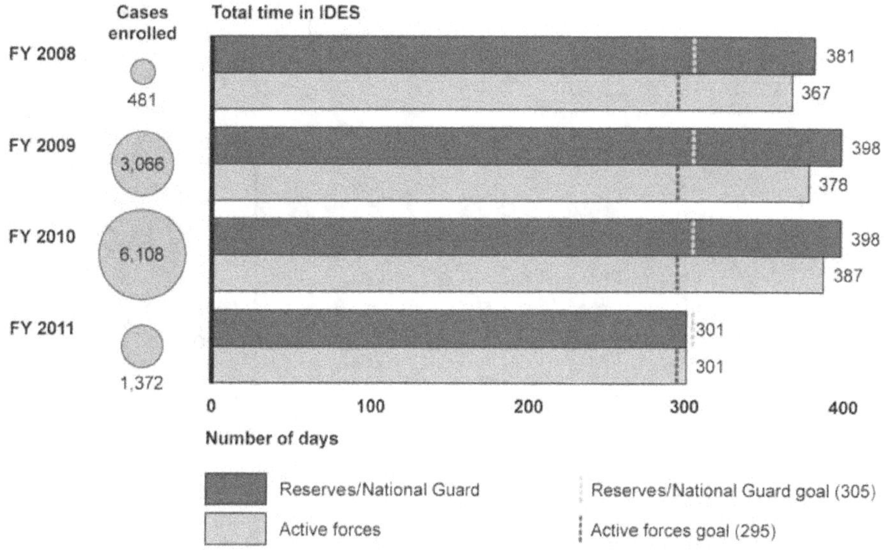

Source: GAO analysis of DOD and VA data.

Note: Enrolled cases reflects those cases that were enrolled for each year with cases with erroneous
or questionable dates removed. This number does not match the number of enrolled cases previously
reported for this reason.

We also examine average IDES processing times according to year of
completion (see fig. 12) and year of enrollment for cases (see fig. 13) for
all completed cases regardless of outcome. As with cases that resulted in
benefits, for cases resulting in any outcome we find that average
processing times increased since 2008—again with the exception of fiscal
year 2011 for reasons discussed earlier—although average processing
times are somewhat shorter than when only servicemembers receiving
benefits are included (fig. 11).

**Figure 12: Average IDES Processing Times by Year of Completion, for All
Completed Cases Regardless of Outcome**

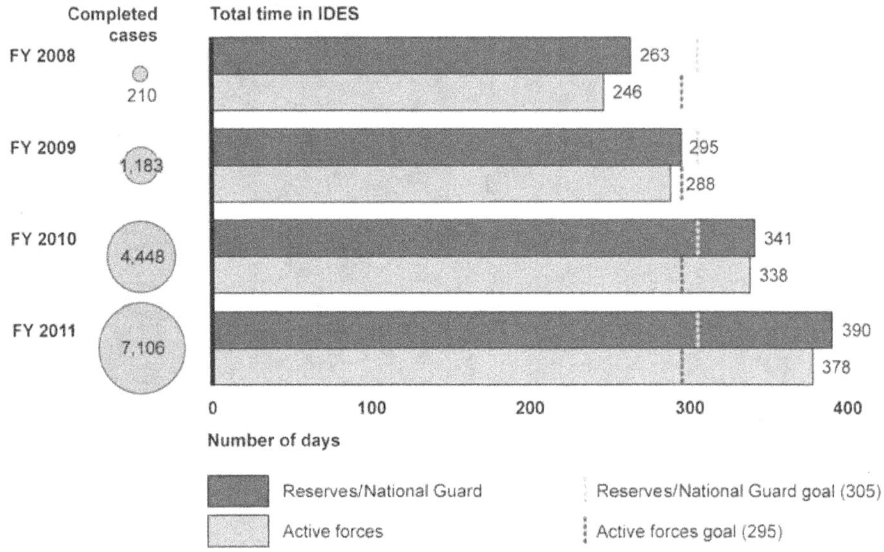

Source: GAO analysis of DOD and VA data.

**Figure 13: Average IDES Processing Times by Fiscal Year of Enrollment for All
Completed Cases Regardless of Outcome**

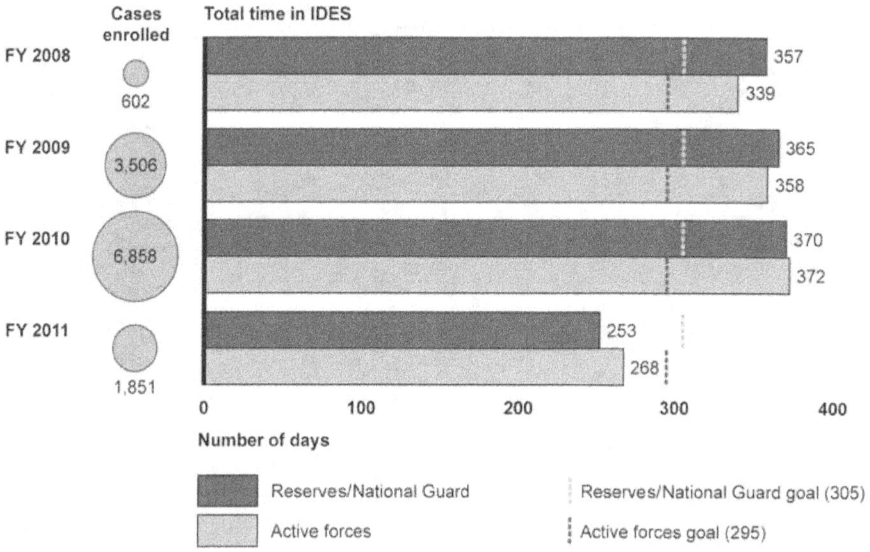

Source: GAO analysis of DOD and VA data.

Note: Enrolled cases reflects those cases that were enrolled for each year with cases with erroneous
or questionable dates removed. This number does not match the number of enrolled cases previously
reported for this reason.

Figures 14 and 15 show that regardless of whether cases are organized
by year of completion or enrollment, the percent of completed cases
resulting in benefits that were not timely increased between fiscal year
2008 and 2010 for both active duty servicemembers and members in the
Reserves or National Guard. As with the average processing times,
caution must be used when examining cases enrolled in fiscal year 2011
(fig. 15), since only those cases that are processed quickly are observed
in the last year. Similarly, caution also must be used when examining
cases in 2008 (fig. 14), since the only cases that are included in the first
year are those that completed IDES quickly.

Figure 14: Percentage of Completed Cases Meeting and Missing the Overall Processing Time Goals, by Fiscal Year of IDES Completion, for Servicemembers Receiving Benefits

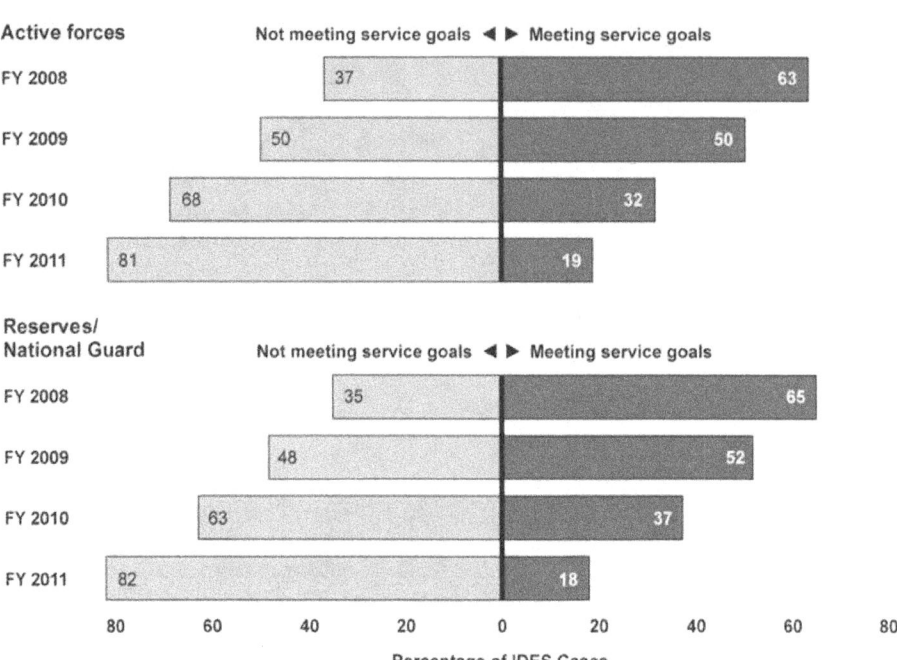

Source: GAO analysis of DOD and VA data.

Figure 15: Percentage of Completed Cases Meeting and Missing the Overall Processing Time Goals, by Fiscal Year of IDES Enrollment, for Servicemembers Receiving Benefits

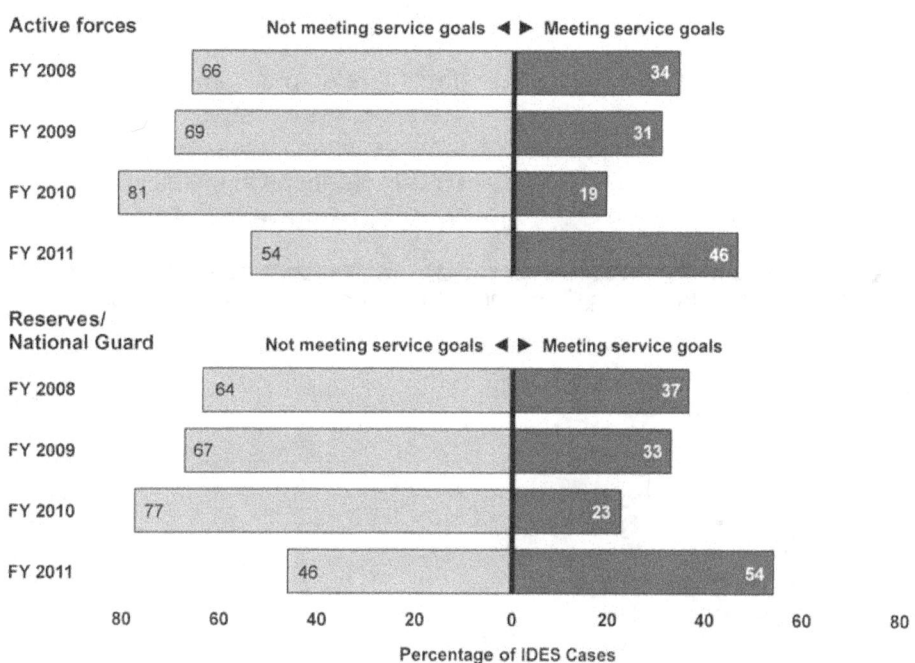

Source: GAO analysis of DOD and VA data.

Figures 16 and 17 show how average processing times for each of the four phases of IDES have changed over the four fiscal years when cases are grouped by the fiscal year in which they completed a given phase and when cases are grouped by the fiscal year in which they were enrolled or started a given phase.[4] Figure 16 shows that when cases are grouped according to the fiscal year in which the different phases were completed, processing times increased for all phases except the Transition phase. Figure 17 shows a roughly similar pattern of increases in processing times in all but the Transition phase, though processing times in 2011 are skewed for the reason mentioned above. Figures 18 and 19 show how the percentages meeting the timeliness goals for each of the four phases of IDES have changed over the four fiscal years when cases are grouped by the fiscal year in which they completed a given phase and when cases

---

[4] The servicemembers included in these figures have not necessarily completed the entire IDES process, but did complete a given phase to be included in the figure for that phase.

are grouped by the fiscal year in which they were enrolled or started a given phase. Figure 18 shows that the percent of cases meeting timeliness goals decreased over the four years for the MEB and PEB phases, although a high percent of cases met PEB goals. However, the Transition and Benefits phases fluctuated up and down and both were favorable across some years. Figure 19 also shows decreases in percentages of cases meeting timeliness goals at the MEB and PEB phases when cases are grouped by fiscal year of starting a given phase. The fluctuations in the timeliness of the Transition and Benefits phases were more prevalent when cases were grouped in this manner.

Figure 16: Average Processing Time for Each IDES Phase, by Fiscal Year in Which the Phase Was Completed

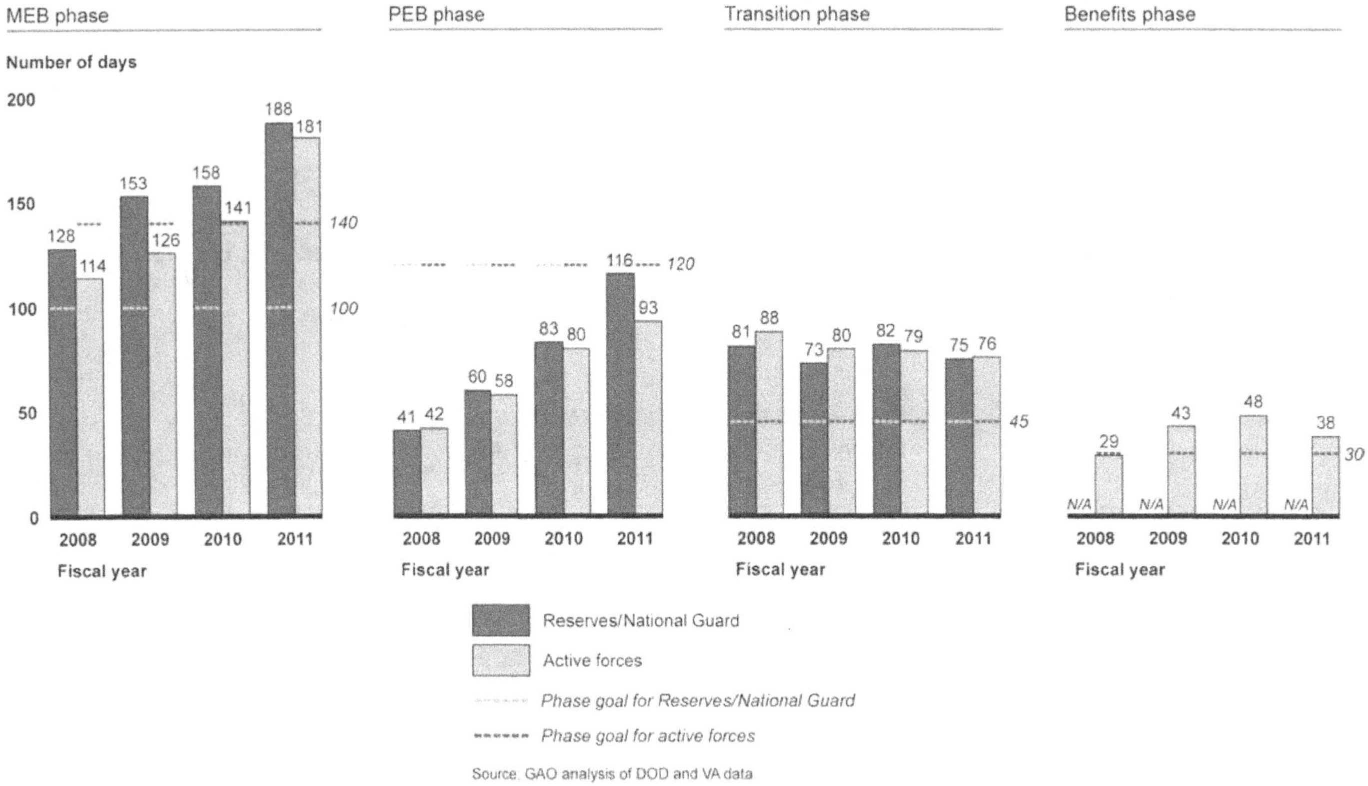

Source: GAO analysis of DOD and VA data

Note: Data shown in figures 16, 17, 18, and 19 are for servicemember cases that either started or completed a phase in a particular year, according to the figure title. For purposes of this report, we opted to not include reserve component time spent in the VA benefit phase in our calculations phase because this goal applies to some but not all reservists, depending on their active duty status. Any time spent within the VA benefit phase is reflected within the overall processing time calculations for such reserve component servicemembers.

Figure 17: Average Processing Time for Each IDES Phase, by Fiscal Year of Enrollment in Each Phase

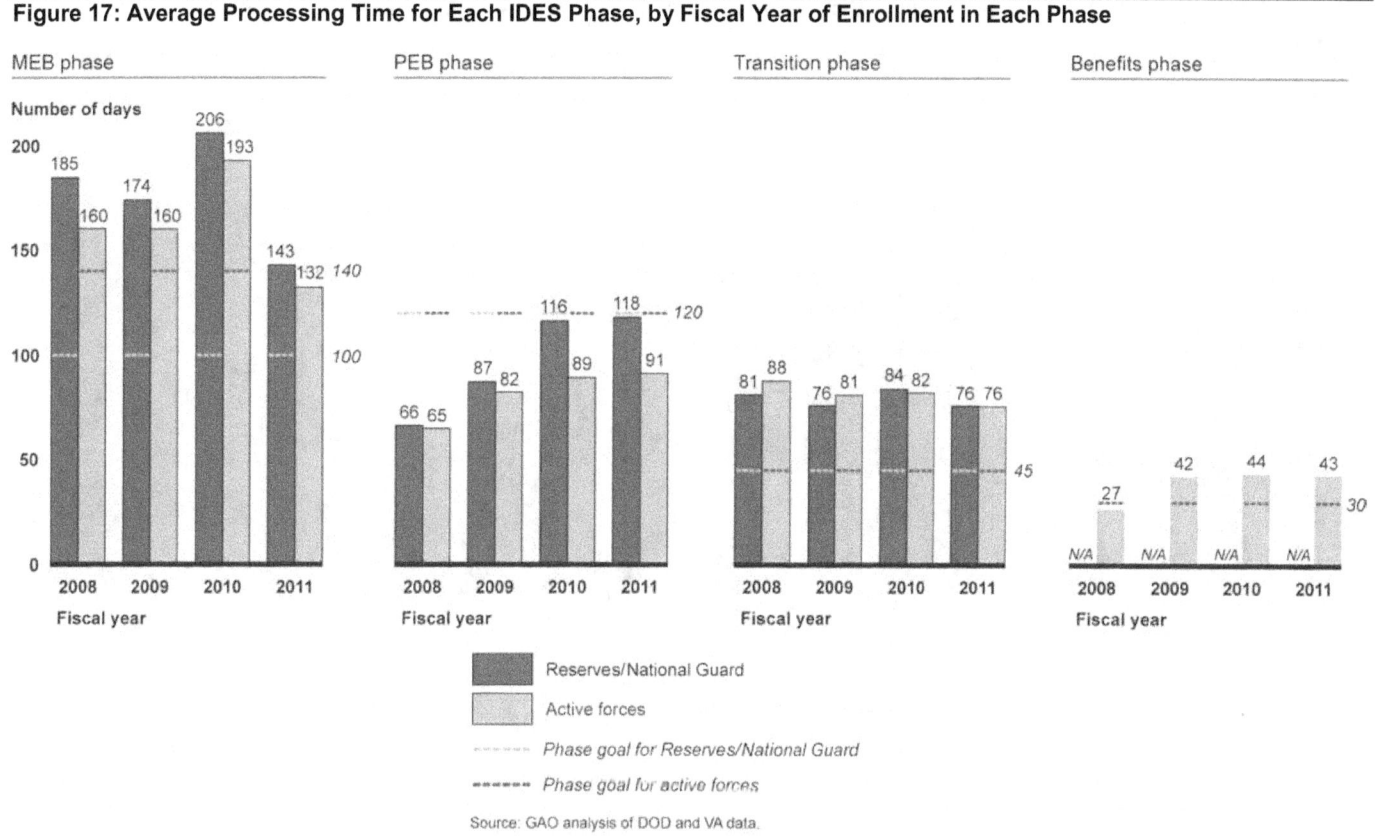

Reserves/National Guard

Active forces

- - - - Phase goal for Reserves/National Guard

------ Phase goal for active forces

Source: GAO analysis of DOD and VA data.

Note: Data shown in figures 16, 17, 18, and 19 are for servicemember cases that either started or completed a phase in a particular year, according to the figure title. For purposes of this report, we opted to not include reserve component time spent in the VA benefit phase in our calculations phase because this goal applies to some but not all reservists, depending on their active duty status. Any time spent within the VA benefit phase is reflected within the overall processing time calculations for such reserve component servicemembers.

Figure 18: Percent of Cases Meeting Timeliness Goals for each Phase of IDES, by Fiscal Year in Which the Phase Was Completed

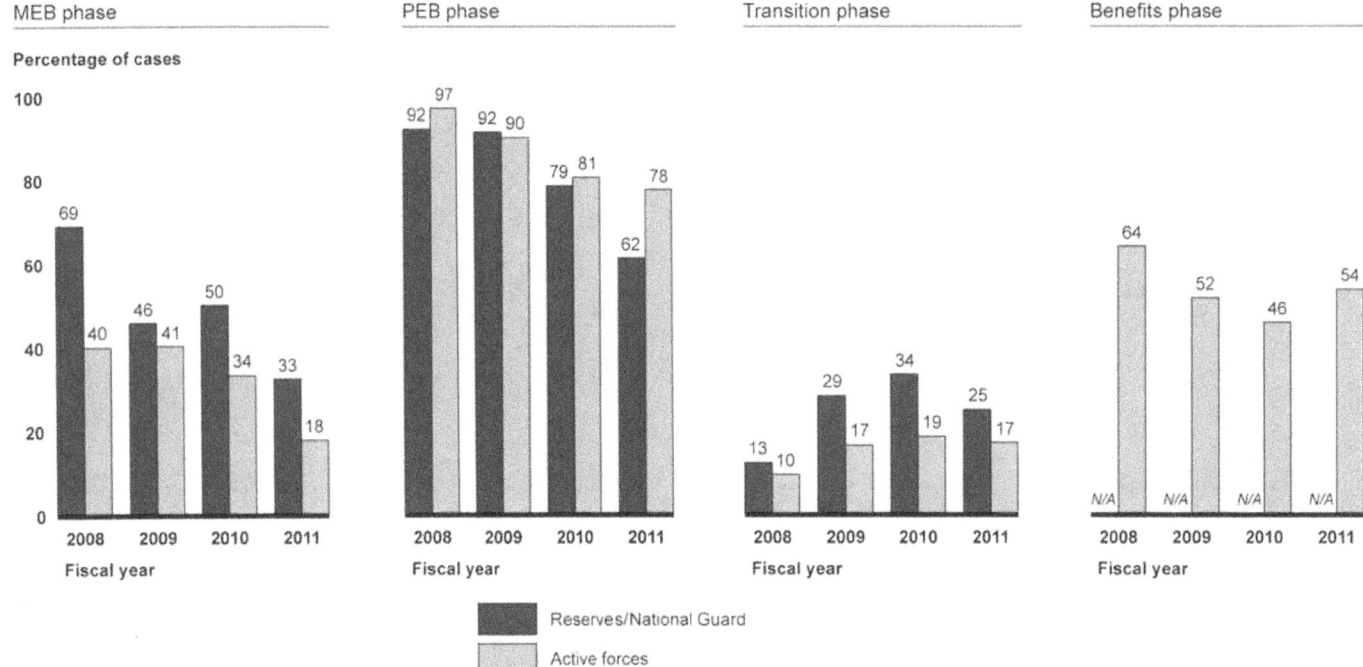

Source: GAO analysis of DOD and VA data.

Note: Data shown in figures 16, 17, 18, and 19 are for servicemember cases that either started or completed a phase in a particular year, according to the figure title. For purposes of this report, we opted to not include reserve component time spent in the VA benefit phase in our calculations phase because this goal applies to some but not all reservists, depending on their active duty status. Any time spent within the VA benefit phase is reflected within the overall processing time calculations for such reserve component servicemembers.

Figure 19: Percent of Cases Meeting Timeliness Goals for each Phase of IDES, by Fiscal Year of Enrollment in Each Phase

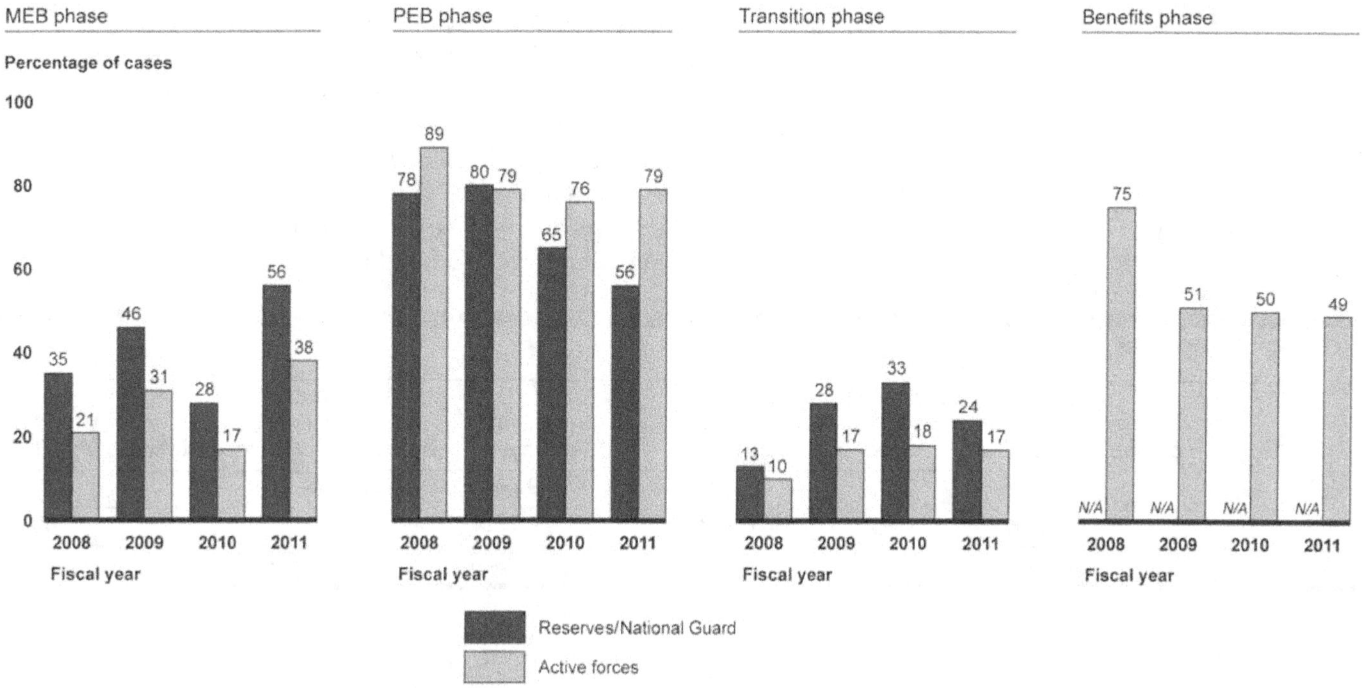

Source: GAO analysis of DOD and VA data

Note: Data shown in figures 16, 17, 18, and 19 are for servicemember cases that either started or completed a phase in a particular year, according to the figure title. For purposes of this report, we opted to not include reserve component time spent in the VA benefit phase in our calculations phase because this goal applies to some but not all reservists, depending on their active duty status. Any time spent within the VA benefit phase is reflected within the overall processing time calculations for such reserve component servicemembers.

Servicemember Satisfaction Survey: Response and Coverage Rates

Low response and coverage rates for servicemember satisfaction surveys administered after each phase of IDES raise concerns about how well the satisfaction survey results represented the larger population of servicemembers who completed one or more phases.

DOD surveys servicemembers after they complete the MEB, PEB, and Transition phases of IDES. The department attempts to survey all servicemembers who complete each phase, but only if they completed the prior surveys. For example, the MEB survey must be completed before a servicemember is eligible to complete the PEB survey.

Using the data available to us, and as table 8 below shows, we found that 9,604 of the 25,212 servicemembers who completed the MEB phase were surveyed, for a 38 percent response and coverage rate.[5] Of the 18,296 servicemembers who completed the PEB phase, only 8,968 of them completed the prior MEB survey and were eligible for the PEB survey and of these only 4,795 were surveyed. Using DOD's eligibility criteria, the response rate for the PEB survey was roughly 54 percent (4,795 of 8,968). However, the coverage rate for all servicemembers who completed the PEB phase (regardless of whether they completed the prior survey) was only 26 percent (4,795 of 18,296). Similarly, the response rate for the Transition survey was 72 percent while the coverage rate was only 23 percent (See table 8).

Table 8: Survey phase response and coverage rates

Phase	Servicemembers completing phase	Servicemembers eligible for survey (completed prior phase survey)	Servicemembers surveyed	Response rate (No. surveyed / No. eligible) (%)	Coverage rate (No. surveyed / No. completing phase) (%)
MEB	25,212	all	9,604	38.1%	38.1%
PEB	18,296	8,968	4,795	53.5%	26.2%
Transition	12,352	3,996	2,893	72.4%	23.4%

Source: GAO analysis of DOD and VA data.

Note: This table excludes 558 cases (or approximately 1.4 percent) of VTA data with logical errors in IDES phase start and end days for any IDES phase (e.g. exclude cases where MEB start date occurs after MEB end date). This table includes the approximately 4 percent of cases we found to have inconsistent start and end dates across phases.

As table 9 below shows, there were some sizable differences between respondents and nonrespondents, especially for the PEB and Transition surveys. For example, respondents to the transition survey spent more time than nonrespondents in the Transition phase, were less likely to be separated with benefits, and were more likely to be placed on the Permanent Disability Retired List. These differences, combined with low response and coverage rates, raise the possibility of biased responses.

---

[5] Though there are different ways to calculate response and coverage rates, which can result in different estimates of these quantities, we chose our response rate and coverage estimates in order to better understand what fraction of the intended group was actually surveyed.

Table 9: Selected Servicemember Characteristics of Respondents and Nonrespondents to the MEB, PEB and Transition Surveys

Survey	Variable	Respondents		Nonrespondents	
		N	Mean or percent	N	Mean or percent
MEB survey	**Timeliness**				
	Total days in MEB	9,604	158.8	15,608	156.6
	Met MEB goal	2,854	29.7%	5,187	33.2%
	Branch				
	Army	5,191	54.1%	8,910	57.1%
	Marine Corps	2,177	22.7%	2,802	18.0%
	Navy	1,417	14.8%	2,168	13.9%
	US Air Force	819	8.5%	1,728	11.1%
	Component				
	Active duty	8,628	89.8%	14,111	90.4%
	Reserve/National Guard	976	10.2%	1,497	9.6%
	Outcome of case				
	Separated with benefits	2,778	31.4%	2,678	31.0%
	Separated without benefits	152	1.7%	134	1.6%
	Permanent disability retirement list	2,191	24.7%	2,192	25.3%
	Temporary disability retirement list	2,704	30.5%	2,730	31.6%
	Found fit and returned to duty	959	10.8%	856	9.9%
	Found unfit and returned to duty	73	0.8%	61	0.7%
PEB Survey	**Timeliness**				
	Total days in PEB	4,764	85.0	13,364	91.2
	Met PEB goal	3,762	79.0%	10,424	78.0%
	Branch				
	Army	2,646	55.5%	8,298	62.1%
	Marine Corps	1,061	22.3%	2,347	17.6%
	Navy	708	14.9%	1,640	12.3%
	US Air Force	349	7.3%	1,079	8.1%
	Component				
	Active duty	4,262	89.5%	12,228	91.5%

Survey	Variable	Respondents		Nonrespondents	
		N	Mean or percent	N	Mean or percent
	Reserve/National Guard	502	10.54	1,136	8.50
	Outcome of case				
	Separated with benefits	1,408	29.6%	4,035	31.9%
	Separated without benefits	72	1.51	211	1.7%
	Permanent disability retirement list	1,222	25.7%	3,147	24.9%
	Temporary disability retirement list	1,440	30.2%	3,962	31.4%
	Found fit and returned to duty	584	12.3%	1,181	9.4%
	Found unfit and returned to duty	38	0.8%	94	0.7%
Transition survey	**Timeliness**				
	Total days in transition	2,894	82.3	9,259	75.1
	Met transition goal	455	15.7%	1,856	20.0%
	Branch				
	Army	1,744	60.3%	5,972	64.5%
	Marine Corps	597	20.6%	1,837	19.8%
	Navy	344	11.9%	924	10.0%
	US Air Force	209	7.2%	526	5.7%
	Component				
	Active Duty	2,587	89.4%	8,562	92.5%
	Reserve/National Guard	307	10.6%	697	7.5%
	Outcome of Case				
	Separated with benefits	783	27.1%	3,496	38.1%
	Separated without benefits	47	1.6%	173	1.9%
	Permanent disability retirement list	955	33.0%	2,405	26.2%
	Temporary disability retirement list	1,102	38.1%	3,086	33.7%
	Found fit and returned to duty	5	0.2%	4	0.0%
	Found unfit and returned to duty	2	0.1%	3	0.0%

Source: GAO analysis of DOD and VA data.

Note: This table excludes 558 cases (or approximately 1.4 percent) of VTA data with logical errors in IDES phase start and end days, for any IDES phase (e.g. exclude cases where MEB start date occurs after MEB end date). This table includes the approximately 4 percent of cases we found to have inconsistent start and end dates across phases.

Measuring Servicemember Satisfaction

The particular measure used to assess servicemember satisfaction can affect the proportion reported as "satisfied" with the IDES program. Depending on the measure used, satisfaction is about 2.8 times lower than what DOD has reported, and many servicemembers classified as "satisfied" express moderate dissatisfaction with some aspects of the process.

DOD has reported average servicemember satisfaction with IDES overall and with three phases of the process, i.e., MEB, PEB, and Transition phases. In so doing, DOD has developed indices of satisfaction on several broad dimensions, such as satisfaction with the overall experience and fairness, which combine responses to selected survey questions. Although the number of questions used in each index vary depending on the number of phases completed, each index classifies servicemembers as "satisfied" or "dissatisfied" using the average of their responses across all questions in the index. Each question's scale ranges from 1 to 5, with 1 denoting "very dissatisfied" (or a similar negative response), 5 denoting "very satisfied," and 3 denoting "neither satisfied nor dissatisfied." DOD reports that a servicemember is "satisfied" if his or her average response across all items in the scale exceeds 3. Table 10 summarizes the responses to each question that DOD uses in its overall satisfaction index at each phase (as of August 2011).

Table 10: Questions Used in DOD Indices of Overall Servicemember Satisfaction

	MEB phase		PEB phase		Transition phase	
	Number	Percent	Number	Percent	Number	Percent
How satisfied or dissatisfied were you with the management of your case during the [MEB/PEB/Transition] phase of the pilot process?						
Very dissatisfied	813	8.4	388	7.9	223	6.4
Dissatisfied	1,369	14.1	607	12.4	406	11.6
Neither	1,259	13	578	11.8	397	11.3
Satisfied	4,310	44.5	2,306	47.1	1,737	49.6
Very satisfied	1,926	19.9	1,019	20.8	741	21.1
Total	**9,677**	**100**	**4,898**	**100**	**3,504**	**100**
How satisfied or dissatisfied were you with the overall [MEB/PEB/Transition] phase of determining your retention status?						
Very dissatisfied	559	6.7	269	5.5	224	6.4
Dissatisfied	1,131	13.6	548	11.2	401	11.5
Neither	1,007	12.1	510	10.4	345	9.9
Satisfied	4,048	48.6	2,562	52.3	1,798	51.6
Very satisfied	1,578	19	1014	20.7	715	20.5
Total	**8,323**	**100**	**4,903**	**100**	**3,483**	**100**
How would you evaluate the timeliness of the process since entering the Disability Evaluation Pilot process?						
Very poor	1,685	17.4	759	15.4	500	14.1
Poor	1,594	16.5	681	13.9	468	13.2
Mix of poor/good	2,397	24.7	1,262	25.7	967	27.3
Good	2,811	29	1,470	29.9	1,065	30.1
Very good	1,200	12.4	743	15.1	543	15.3
Total	**9,687**	**100**	**4,915**	**100**	**3,543**	**100**
How would you evaluate your overall experience since entering the Disability Evaluation Pilot process?						
Very poor	686	7	356	7.2	235	6.6
Poor	921	9.4	413	8.4	285	8
Mix of poor/good	2,875	29.4	1,477	29.9	1,115	31.4
Good	3,891	39.8	1,917	38.8	1,333	37.5
Very good	1,402	14.3	772	15.6	587	16.5
Total	**9,775**	**100**	**4,935**	**100**	**3,555**	**100**

Source: GAO analysis of DOD data.

Note: Entries are responses to four survey questions (rows) asked after servicemembers complete the MEB, PEB, or Transition phase (columns).

DOD's indices are one reasonable method of summarizing
servicemember opinions. In quarterly performance reports, DOD notes
that it has used factor analysis, a form of latent variable statistical models
to assess the reliability of its scales. While we did not review DOD's
models, we independently found that DOD's overall index of satisfaction
with IDES was highly reliable. (Specifically, using Cronbach's alpha, the
index was highly correlated with a single latent dimension at $\alpha = 0.92$.)
This supports DOD's choice to measure the single concept of
"satisfaction" by averaging the ordinal servicemember responses.

Nevertheless, the average survey response can obscure variation in the
responses that make up the index. For example, suppose that a
servicemember said she was "very satisfied" (response of 5) on two of the
four questions in the index, "dissatisfied" on one (response of 2) and "very
dissatisfied" on the last one (response of 1). With an average response
over 3, the DOD measure would classify her as "satisfied," despite the
fact that she was "somewhat dissatisfied" or "very dissatisfied" with two of
the four aspects of IDES that DOD considers important. The grouping rule
considers this servicemember equally happy with IDES as someone who
says they are "satisfied" with all four aspects in the index.

To assess the extent to which DOD's index might mask dissatisfaction,
we calculated the proportion of questions in the scale on which
servicemembers whom DOD classified as "satisfied" gave neutral or
negative responses (1, 2, or 3). We found that half of these
servicemembers gave neutral or negative answers to at least 25 percent
of the items in the index, and a quarter gave such answers to at least 41
percent of the items. For these servicemembers, the DOD index may
suggest more satisfaction than the underlying survey questions would
support.

We further assessed the sensitivity of DOD's index by comparing it
against a different (i.e., GAO's) measure of satisfaction: whether a
servicemember is "somewhat" or "very satisfied" (or gives a similarly
positive response) on all items in DOD's scale of overall IDES
satisfaction. Our measure is more conservative than DOD's, because
ours only includes positive responses and uses a broader cutpoint (two
response categories) to distinguish between "satisfied" and "not satisfied"
servicemembers. (In contrast, DOD calculates average satisfaction on an
ordinal scale of 1 to 5, and then uses a cutpoint at 3.) Our measure is not

inherently more valid, however, and has its own weaknesses. In
particular, we classify a servicemember as "not satisfied" if she gives a
neutral or negative response to just one of the four items in DOD's scale.[6]

When we analyzed overall satisfaction using both measures, we found
that overall, servicemembers are 2.8 times less satisfied on our measure
than on DOD's (i.e., 23.8 versus 67 percent). Further, only about 20 to 30
percent of servicemembers are "satisfied" with each aspect of the IDES
process that DOD considers important across most of the subgroups we
analyzed, while DOD classifies about 60 to 70 percent of such
servicemembers as "satisfied" on average. In the next section, we present
further information on variation in satisfaction across servicemember
groups.

Explaining Servicemember Satisfaction Outcomes

Although the servicemember survey provides numerous measures of
satisfaction, it is also important to explain variation in satisfaction
outcomes—i.e. why some servicemembers are more satisfied than
others. Explaining variation can connect dissatisfaction with poor program
performance and help identify specific reforms to improve the
experiences of servicemembers who typically have been less satisfied.
However, the available program data cannot precisely explain outcomes
when used in this type of explanatory analysis. Using the available data,
we could predict satisfaction only 1.9 percentage points better after
controlling for multiple factors than what we would have achieved by
chance (65.5 percent vs. 63.7 percent of satisfied responses predicted
correctly).

In order to further explain variation in satisfaction, we matched the survey
responses to the data that DOD and VA maintain on the processing of
each servicemember's case, known as the VTA data. This database
primarily measures the time it took servicemembers to complete each
phase of the IDES process. A small number of other program and
demographic variables are also available, such as service branch,

---

[6] Both measures of satisfaction combine responses from servicemembers who have
finished various phases of IDES. For example, a servicemember who completed only the
MEB would provide at most 4 responses from that wave's survey, while a servicemember
who completed all phases would provide at most 12 responses from all three surveys.
Each measure calculates overall satisfaction using all responses available, even though
the number of responses varies among servicemembers (e.g., 4 vs. 12).

component, and the number of conditions claimed and referred. Using the matched survey and VTA data, we estimated the association between satisfaction and observable factors that could potentially explain variation in servicemembers' experiences.

Table 11 below (columns 2-4) presents these associations for both DOD's and GAO's overall measures of satisfaction. The "raw data" estimates are simply the proportion of servicemembers in a particular group who were satisfied according to either measure. In the fourth column ("model estimates"), we estimate this proportion holding constant all of the other factors listed, using a statistical model. Specifically, the estimates are in-sample mean predicted probabilities of giving a satisfied response on the GAO satisfaction index from a logistic model of satisfaction. The covariates are given by indicators of whether the servicemember belonged to each group in column 4. The maximum likelihood estimators allowed the probability of satisfaction, given the covariates, to be dependent across observations within the 26 cross-classified groups of PEB location and MEB medical treatment facility. This adjusted for the possibility that servicemembers were similarly satisfied if they were processed in the same locations, given similar values on the observed covariates.[7]

Table 11: Overall IDES Satisfaction by Subgroups

	DOD Measure: Average answer exceeded neutral	GAO Measure: All answers positive		
	Raw data	Raw data	Model estimates	
	Percentage	Percentage	Percentage	N
All respondents	67	23.8		9,865
Component				
Active	67.4	23.7	23.7	8,692
Reserves/National Guard	63.5	24.6	23.7	1,173

[7] Because the "cluster-robust" variance estimator is only consistent as the number of clusters becomes large, the relatively small number of MEB-PEB locations in our data raises the possibility of finite-sample bias. The practical effect of this problem should be minimal, however, since the model controls for MEB and PEB location and, thus, residual intraclass correlation should be small.

	DOD Measure: Average answer exceeded neutral	GAO Measure: All answers positive		
	Raw data	Raw data	Model estimates	
	Percentage	Percentage	Percentage	N
Branch				
Air Force	61.8	23.6	23.7	838
Army	70.3	26.5	24.5	5,398
Marine Corps	61.3	19	23.8	2,198
Navy	65.9	21.2	23	1,431
Rollout phase[a]				
1	63.7	20.2		1,430
1.1	65.1	21.8		4,827
2	72.7	30.4		1,601
3.1	69.6	34.6		257
3.2	67.7	38.5		65
3.3	0	0		1
Final disposition				
Fit and Returned to Duty	70.9	27.4	21.7	963
Permanent Disability Retirement List	69.9	25.4	25.6	2,286
Separated with Benefits	66.9	23.1	22.5	2,848
Separated without Benefits	63.1	20.4	21.5	157
Temporary Disability Retirement List	65.9	21.8	24.4	2,786
Unfit and Returned to Duty	63	16.4	17	73
Fiscal Year started MEB				
2008	60.4	15.1	13	530
2009	68.1	21.4	21.2	2,627
2010	66.1	22.9	24.5	4,721
2011	69.3	31.6	28.3	1,986
Claimed conditions				
0-4	71.5	27.7	24.2	2,309
5-7	69.4	25.1	23.9	2,028
8-12	65.9	22.5	23.1	2,771
13-19	62.6	22.6	25.1	1,882
20+	61.7	16.6	20.2	825

	DOD Measure: Average answer exceeded neutral	GAO Measure: All answers positive		
	Raw data	Raw data	Model estimates	
	Percentage	Percentage	Percentage	N
Referred conditions				
0-1	67.7	24.9	24.1	4,686
2	66.1	24	23.7	2,482
3	65.8	21.6	23.4	1,679
4+	67.8	22.5	22	953
DOD Percentage Rating				
0	66.5	20.8		236
10	67.3	24.6		1,287
20	66.6	23.1		978
30	67.1	23.7		680
40	67.2	22.2		531
50	65.4	21.5		786
60	66.7	23		609
70	68.2	21.2		556
80	68.9	30		280
90	63.1	21.3		122
100	75.5	35.5		282
MEB treatment facility				
Andrews	57.4	18.5	19.8	319
Lejeune	56.9	18	18.4	1,046
Pendleton	62.1	17	19.2	372
Belvoir	66.3	25	30.1	252
Benning	77.3	34	25.6	260
Bliss				0
Bragg	72.9	36.8	34.3	288
Campbell	90	50	47	10
Carson	64.3	19	23.7	736
Drum	67.3	30	27.9	397
Gordon	50	50		2
Hood	81.1	33.3	30.7	519
Lewis	59.5	21	20.2	252
Meade	55.5	15.6	14.7	218
Polk	81	33.3	28.1	400

	DOD Measure: Average answer exceeded neutral	GAO Measure: All answers positive		
	Raw data	Raw data	Model estimates	
	Percentage	Percentage	Percentage	N
Riley	59	20	17.4	105
Stewart	74.2	26.7	27	718
Other	68	25.6	20.3	961
Portsmouth	65	23	21.8	283
San Antonio	71.1	26.3	24.2	505
San Diego	65.2	20.5	21.3	1,127
Tripler	83.3	53	37.8	30
Walter Reed (Army)	65.2	21.7	26.4	511
Walter Reed (Navy/Marine Corps)	66.4	19.9	24.1	554
Time in IDES (GAO calculation) at disenrollment or December 31, 2011)				
1st quartile	81.5	38.3	41.1	313
2nd quartile	78.2	35	33.8	1,658
3rd quartile	70.1	24.8	23.7	3,667
4th quartile	58.8	17.4	17.8	4,226
Sex				
Female	66.9	25.4	25.2	1,799
Male	67	23.5	23.3	8,063
Personnel Class				
Enlisted	67.1	23.9	23.9	9,126
Officer	64.5	21.7	21	691
Warrant	77	29.2	27.6	48
PEB Location				
Lewis	64.2	20.4		1,283
National Capital Region	66	26.1		1,698
San Antonio (Randolph)	61.8	23.6		838
San Antonio (Sam Houston)	76.5	30		2,417
Washington Navy Yard	63.1	19.9		3,629
MEB Exam Location				
Military Treatment Facility	67.2	24.1	22.1	868

	DOD Measure: Average answer exceeded neutral	GAO Measure: All answers positive		
	Raw data	Raw data	Model estimates	
	Percentage	Percentage	Percentage	N
Contractor Facility	67	23.9	23.7	1,991
VA Medical Center	66.9	24.2	23.4	5,976
Not Available	66.9	21.2	27.2	1,030

Source: GAO analysis of DOD and VA data.

[a]Rollout phases correspond with the order in which IDES deployed at various facilities.

Regardless of which measure is used (DOD's or GAO's), satisfaction varied only modestly across many important groups of servicemembers. Our model estimates that the GAO measure of satisfaction varied by no more than approximately five percentage points across branch, component, disenrollment outcome, sex, MEB exam provider, enlisted and officer personnel classes, and the number of claimed and referred conditions, although differences across MEB treatment facilities and PEB locations were larger.[8] This can be seen as a positive outcome, if this correlation implies that DOD and VA administer the program consistently across servicemembers and locations. However, the lack of variation also could suggest that the survey items do not measure opinions in enough detail to discriminate among servicemembers' experiences.

Also shown in table 11, satisfaction had a stronger association with case processing time (time spent in IDES) than some of the other factors we examined. Servicemembers whose case processing times were among the quickest 25 percent were about 2.3 times as likely to be satisfied (on the GAO scale) than those whose times were among the 25 percent of cases with the longest overall timeframes (i.e., 41 versus 18 percent). Nevertheless, only 41 percent of those servicemembers whose cases were processed most quickly were satisfied (holding constant the other factors). This suggests that servicemembers' opinions about IDES may be only loosely related to the amount of time they spent in IDES, as discussed in the next section below.

---

[8] In addition, servicemembers who were found unfit and returned to duty—a rare outcome—were approximately 4 to 10 percentage points less likely to be satisfied than servicemembers who had any of the other outcomes.

Although the average case processing time has generally increased since 2008, when we look at satisfaction by fiscal year, servicemember satisfaction shows evidence of improvement since fiscal year 2008. Specifically, our measure of satisfaction from the model increased by 15 percentage points since 2008, roughly doubling from 13 to 28. Because the model estimates control for various other factors, these results suggest that servicemember views of the IDES process have improved over time, rather than the possibility that IDES has simply processed different types of cases.

Satisfaction does not vary by a large amount across many MEB treatment facilities, but there are exceptions. Our model estimates that about 18 to 26 percent of servicemembers were satisfied at most facilities. However, there were pockets of greater satisfaction. Specifically, servicemembers had more positive experiences at Forts Belvoir, Bragg, Campbell, Drum, Hood, and Polk, with satisfaction estimated to have ranged from 28 to 45 percentage points. Fort Meade had the lowest satisfaction at 15 percent. These estimates hold constant time spent in IDES and other factors in column 4 and, thus, partially account for the types of cases each facility processes.

Satisfaction with Timeliness

DOD and VA measure IDES timeliness directly in VTA and as part of the overall servicemember satisfaction scale. These overlapping measures let us compare servicemembers' opinions to their actual experiences in the program. To do this, we calculated processing times at each phase of IDES for servicemembers who expressed varying degrees of satisfaction with the timeliness of their case processing at that phase. In addition, we analyzed whether servicemembers who were satisfied with the overall IDES process were more or less likely to meet timeliness goals. Table 12 provides these statistics.

Table 12: Perceived Timeliness of IDES by Actual Processing Times

	Days in IDES (by phase)			Actual processing time (by Phase)				% Met DOD Goal	N
	10th Pctile	Median	90th Pctile	% in 1st Quartile	% in 2nd Quartile	% in 3rd Quartile	% in 4th Quartile		
Overall satisfaction with IDES (GAO Measure)									
Not satisfied	198	348	544	2.57	14.33	36.68	46.42	33.8	7,516
Satisfied	159	297	479	5.11	24.74	38.76	31.39	50.2	2,349
Perceived MEB timeliness									
Very poor	88	175	323	7.9	22.5	30.9	38.7	16.8	1,685
Poor	78	156	290	11.6	25.7	35.1	27.6	23.4	1,594
Mix of poor/good	72	142	273	15.1	28.6	34.7	21.6	27.9	2,397
Good	66	128	254	19.8	31.9	29.8	18.6	35.6	2,811
Very good	62	114	223	24.9	38.2	24.3	12.6	45.3	1,200
Perceived PEB timeliness satisfaction									
Very poor	28	88	203	22.8	18.1	23.7	35.4	67.8	759
Poor	28	89	186	20.8	18.9	24.7	35.7	69.7	680
Mix of poor/good	23	70	155	28.3	23.4	24	24.3	79.5	1,262
Good	23	65	138	30.7	25.5	24.4	19.4	84.3	1,470
Very good	17	55	128	40.2	26.2	18	15.6	88.1	740
Perceived Transition timeliness									
Very poor	33	87	461	7.9	22.5	30.9	38.7	16.1	500
Poor	43	90	459	11.6	25.7	35.1	27.6	12.6	468
Mix of poor/good	40	90	481	15.1	28.6	34.7	21.6	13.3	967
Good	37	91	496	19.8	31.9	29.8	18.6	12.8	1,065
Very good	39	91	657	24.9	38.2	24.3	12.6	12.8	541

Source: GAO analysis of DOD and VA data.

As shown in table 12, satisfaction generally stayed the same or decreased as processing times increased. The median days spent in the MEB and PEB phases were 35 and 38 percent lower, respectively, among those servicemembers who said that MEB and PEB timeliness was "very good" as compared to those who said it was "very poor." The former group was 170 percent more likely to have met the MEB timeliness goal and 30 percent more likely to have met the PEB timeliness goal. Similarly, the case for a median servicemember—whom we classified as "satisfied" with the overall IDES process—was completed 15 percent more quickly and was 49 percent more likely to have met the timeliness goal than the median servicemember who was "dissatisfied." The model estimates in table 11 confirm that the GAO measure of satisfaction and timeliness (time spent in IDES) are negatively related even when holding constant several other variables.

Perceived and actual timeliness had little association at the Transition phase. Across all levels of satisfaction with timeliness, the median processing time varied by no more than 4 days, and the proportion meeting the timeliness goal varied by no more than 4 percentage points. The use of personal leave is one plausible explanation for the unresponsiveness of servicemember satisfaction to actual processing times in the Transition phase. A servicemember might not have been dissatisfied with delays if taking leave was the reason, rather than the IDES process itself.

Despite the associations between actual and perceived timeliness at the MEB and PEB phases, there were many servicemembers who were satisfied or dissatisfied with timeliness that spent similar amounts of time in the program. For example, 68 percent of those who said that PEB timeliness was "very poor" completed the phase on time, and 55 percent of those who said that MEB timeliness was "very good" did not complete on time. Among servicemembers who said that MEB timeliness was "very good," the middle 80 percent of processing times ranged from 62 days to 223 days. The same range for servicemembers who said MEB timeliness was "very poor" was 88 to 323 days. As table 12 shows, a similar pattern holds for the PEB phase. Although servicemembers tend to be more satisfied in MEB and PEB when their cases take less time, many of them are highly dissatisfied even when their cases take an unusually short amount of time (and vice versa). In the Transition phase, however, 40 percent of servicemembers who said that timeliness was "very good" were processed in 91 to 657 days—a more lengthy range than at the other phases. The large range and relationship with satisfaction may reflect the use of servicemember leave.

The fact that many servicemembers are similarly satisfied with timeliness, even though they can have widely different processing times, has broader implications for measuring the performance of IDES. DOD's timeliness goals may not be meaningful to servicemembers or necessarily reflect high-quality service. Alternatively, servicemembers may not use reasonable standards to assess the time required to process their cases, or they may not accurately perceive the time they have spent in the program. In these scenarios, the value of servicemember satisfaction as a performance measure becomes less certain.

The relationship between perceived and actual timeliness may simply reflect a large amount of unobserved heterogeneity across servicemembers. For example, a servicemember whose case has been in IDES for an extremely long time might still be highly satisfied with timeliness if the case was complex or personal leave was taken during the process. Neither the survey nor the VTA data measure these or other such characteristics that might affect the program's key performance measures.

Factors Affecting Survey Results and Implications for Program Evaluation

The lack of variation in satisfaction across servicemember groups and according case timeliness might be seen as a positive outcome, and may suggest that DOD and VA administer the program consistently across servicemembers and locations. However, the lack of variation also could suggest shortcomings in the design and administration of the survey, or in data limitations that, alone or together, may reduce the usefulness of survey data for program evaluation. For example:

- *Survey questions*: The survey questions may not be sufficiently detailed to measure important differences among servicemembers' experiences. For example, the survey includes 12 questions (4 per survey) that measure broad opinions about IDES, and DOD subsequently averages these responses together. This approach may limit the survey's capacity to describe IDES experiences in sufficient detail.

- *Precision of DOD indices*: DOD reports measures of overall satisfaction with IDES for each phase, using the questions in table 9. However, these measures include one question that asks respondents to "evaluate their overall experience since entering the IDES process," which could be influenced by experiences in prior phases. Consequently, the satisfaction measures reported for each phase could represent a combination of servicemembers' experiences in that phase and prior phases.

- *Completing two surveys at once*: DOD officials told us that a servicemember may be surveyed for the PEB and Transition phases in one session. In these instances a large amount of time may have passed since the servicemember completed the PEB phase and it may be more difficult for the servicemember to isolate his or her satisfaction with a particular phase.

- *Survey design*: The satisfaction survey is primarily designed to measure performance, not explain it. The survey includes many highly correlated questions measuring satisfaction with the overall process or broad components of it, such as DOD board liaisons, VA case managers, or timeliness. While multiple questions can improve the statistical reliability and validity of DOD's performance measures, they require costly survey administration time that could be used for other purposes, such as to measure a larger number of variables that could explain servicemember satisfaction or case processing times.

- *VTA data limitations*: The VTA administrative data that we matched to survey data primarily measure processing times and basic servicemember demographics, such as service branch, component, and treatment facility. The data support detailed reporting of performance measures, but they do not measure similarly detailed information on the nature of each case that might allow DOD and VA to understand the reasons for lengthy case processing times or to identify cases that might become delayed and ensure that they remain on schedule. For example, the database does not measure the type or severity of referred medical conditions in detail, the nature of delays experienced early in the process, or the use of servicemember leave. In addition, little information is available on staffing at or caseloads for MEB and PEB locations, DOD board liaisons, or VA case managers, which might help to explain or predict performance.

- *Low response and coverage rates*: The response and coverage rates of the satisfaction survey further limit the degree to which DOD can generalize the data obtained to the population of servicemembers who participate in IDES. In particular, the survey does not assess the views of servicemembers who disenroll from the process before finishing a stage or those who do not complete prior waves of the survey. Including servicemembers who do not complete all waves would complicate longitudinal analysis, however.

Appendix III: Monthly DOD Timeliness Data for Active Duty Cases in Fiscal Year 2012

Table 13 presents data reported by DOD on average processing time for active duty cases completed during part of fiscal year 2012—Oct. 2011 to June 2012. DOD's data are provided as a supplement the analyses GAO conducted for fiscal years 2008 through 2011.[1] We did not evaluate the reliability of these data and cannot predict the extent to which any trends will continue for the rest of the fiscal year.

Table 13: DOD Reported Monthly Average Processing Times for Active Component Servicemembers in Fiscal Year 2012 (in days)

Time spent in:	Goal (days)	Month that IDES process, phase or stage was completed								
		Oct. 2011	Nov. 2011	Dec. 2011	Jan. 2012	Feb. 2012	Mar. 2012	Apr. 2012	May 2012	June 2012
IDES overall (only cases resulting in receipt of benefits)	295	395	391	404	395	392	394	400	409	395
MEB phase	100	136	130	128	132	130	124	114	116	122
Medical Exam Stage	45	40	39	41	44	37	37	39	39	39
MEB Stage	35	76	71	73	76	77	72	64	66	69
PEB phase	120	95	100	104	112	116	111	114	120	122
Informal PEB stage	15	23	28	34	34	28	23	22	19	24
VA Preliminary Rating stage	15	26	27	31	34	3/	51	58	45	35
Transition phase	45	71	70	69	75	77	76	74	77	74
VA Benefits phase	30	38	36	47	56	49	50	57	66	62

Source: DOD IDES Monthly Reports for April, May June , and July 2012.

Note: This table does not reflect data on all phases or stages of the IDES process. Instead, it presents data on those phases and stages that GAO also presented data on in the body of the report.

---

[1] DOD calculates timeliness separately for active, reserve, and guard components. Because our report includes analysis for active and reserve/guard combined, we are only including active servicemembers in this appendix for easy comparison. Active duty cases reflect the bulk of cases in fiscal year 2012, as with other fiscal years.

Appendix IV: Comments from the Department of Defense

OFFICE OF THE ASSISTANT SECRETARY OF DEFENSE

WASHINGTON, DC 20301-1200

HEALTH AFFAIRS

Mr. Daniel Bertoni
Director, Education, Workforce, and Income Security Issues
U.S. Government Accountability Office
441 G Street, NW
Washington, DC 20548

Dear Mr. Bertoni,

This is the Department of Defense (DoD) response to the Government Accountability Office (GAO) Draft Report 12-676, "MILITARY DISABILITY SYSTEM: Improved Monitoring Needed to Better Track and Manage Performance," July 18, 2012 (GAO Code 131089).

While the Department notes inaccuracy in some content of the report in regard to Veteran surveys, we concur with the GAO's three recommendations. The DoD response is attached to this letter.

Sincerely,

John R. Campbell
Deputy Assistance Secretary of Defense for
Warrior Care Policy

GAO DRAFT REPORT DATED JULY 18, 2012
GAO-12-676 (GAO CODE 131089)

"MILITARY DISABILITY SYSTEM: IMPROVED MONITORING NEEDED TO
BETTER TRACK AND MANAGE PERFORMANCE"

DEPARTMENT OF DEFENSE COMMENTS
TO THE GAO RECOMMENDATIONS

RECOMMENDATION 1: To ensure that Service member cases are processed and are
awarded benefits in a timely manner, we recommend that the Secretaries of Defense and
Veterans Affairs work together to develop timeframes for completing the IDES business
process review and implementing any resulting recommendations.

DoD RESPONSE: Concur.

RECOMMENDATION 2: To improve DOD's ability to measure Service members'
satisfaction with the IDES process, we recommend that the Secretary of Defense develop
alternative approaches for collecting more meaningful and representative information in a
cost effective manner.

DoD RESPONSE: Concur.

RECOMMENDATION 3: To ensure that IDES management decisions continue to be
based upon reliable and accurate data, we recommend that the Secretaries of Defense and
Veterans Affairs work together to develop a strategy to continuously monitor and remedy
issues with VTA timeliness information. This could include issuing guidance to facilities
or developing best practices on preventing and correcting data entry errors; and
developing reporting capabilities in VTA to alert facilities to potential issues with their
data.

DoD RESPONSE: Concur.

Appendix V: Comments from the Department of Veterans Affairs

DEPARTMENT OF VETERANS AFFAIRS
Washington DC 20420

August 20, 2012

Mr. Daniel B. Bertoni
Director
Education, Workforce, and
  Income Security Issues
U.S. Government Accountability Office
441 G Street, NW
Washington, DC 20548

Dear Mr. Bertoni:

The Department of Veterans Affairs (VA) has reviewed the Government Accountability Office's (GAO) draft report, *"MILITARY DISABILITY SYSTEM: Improved Monitoring Needed to Better Track and Manage Performance"* (GAO-12-676) and concurs with Recommendations 1 and 3 made to the Department. The enclosure contains additional details on VA's planned actions to address both recommendations, and technical comments to the draft report.

VA appreciates the opportunity to comment on your draft report.

Sincerely,

John R. Gingrich
Chief of Staff

Enclosure

Department of Veterans Affairs (VA) Comments to
Government Accountability Office (GAO) Draft Report
**"MILITARY DISABILITY SYSTEM: Improved Monitoring Needed
to Better Track and Manage Performance"**
(GAO-12-676)

GAO Recommendation 1: **To ensure that servicemember cases are processed
and are awarded benefits in a timely manner, we recommend that the Secretaries
of Defense and Veterans Affairs work together to develop timeframes for
completing the IDES business process review and implementing any resulting
recommendations.**

VA Response: Concur. Although the Department of Defense (DoD) has been leading
the business process review efforts described in this report, the Department of Veterans
Affairs (VA) has provided input and support to promote these efforts and will continue to
do so to the extent possible. At this time, the full scope or current status of these efforts
has not been disclosed to VA. As such, VA recommends that developing timeframes
for completion of these efforts should be deferred to DoD. If, as a result of these
business process reviews, recommendations are set forth and approved by VA and
DoD, VA will contribute to the development of timeframes for implementation of these
recommendations.

GAO Recommendation 3: **To ensure that IDES management decisions continue
to be based upon reliable and accurate data, we recommend that the Secretaries
and Defense and Veterans Affairs work together to develop a strategy to
continuously monitor and remedy issues with VTA timeliness information. This
could include issuing guidance to facilities or developing best practices on
preventing and correcting data entry errors; and developing reporting capabilities
in VTA to alert facilities to potential issues with their data.**

VA Response: Concur. VA is currently engaged in several efforts to improve the
quality of Veterans Tracking Application (VTA) data. VA now leads bi-monthly VTA
training sessions, which are offered to both VA and DoD users. The training serves as
an introduction for new users and refresher training for experienced users. As VA
identifies error trends in VTA data, the training is modified to address those trends.
Further, VA holds a monthly Integrated Disability Evaluation System (IDES)
teleconference call for IDES field personnel. As part of this call, VTA updates are
shared each month, including information about system updates, reminders (to address
error trends), and best practices (to facilitate compliance). Finally, during routine
oversight visits of regional offices and intake sites, VA conducts IDES program reviews
that include verifying the timeliness and accuracy of VTA data entered by VA users.

VA continues to identify VTA reporting capability needs and will examine the feasibility
of alerting local users of potential outlier data. Expected date of completion, to include
VTA programming, is September 30, 2014.

Appendix VI: GAO Contact and Staff Acknowledgments

GAO Contact	Daniel Bertoni, (202) 512-7215, bertonid@gao.gov
Staff Acknowledgments	Michele Grgich (Assistant Director), Daniel Concepcion, Melissa Jaynes, and Greg Whitney made significant contributions to all aspects of this report. Also contributing to this report were Bonnie Anderson, James Bennett, Mark Bird, Joanna Chan, Brenda Farrell, Jamila Jones Kennedy, Douglas Sloane, Almeta Spencer, Vanessa Taylor, Jeffrey Tessin, Roger Thomas, Walter Vance, Kathleen van Gelder, and Sonya Vartivarian.

Related GAO Products

Military Disability System: Preliminary Observations on Efforts to Improve Performance. GAO-12-718T (Washington, D.C.: May 23, 2012).

Military and Veterans Disability System: Worldwide Deployment of Integrated System Warrants Careful Monitoring. GAO-11-633T (Washington, D.C.: May 4, 2011).

Military and Veterans Disability System: Pilot Has Achieved Some Goals, but Further Planning and Monitoring Needed. GAO-11-69 (Washington, D.C.: December 6, 2010).

Military and Veterans Disability System: Preliminary Observations on Evaluation and Planned Expansion of DOD/VA Pilot. GAO-11-191T (Washington, D.C.: November 18, 2010).

Veterans' Disability Benefits: Further Evaluation of Ongoing Initiatives Could Help Identify Effective Approaches for Improving Claims Processing. GAO-10-213 (Washington, D.C.: January 29, 2010).

Recovering Servicemembers: DOD and VA Have Jointly Developed the Majority of Required Policies but Challenges Remain. GAO-09-728 (Washington, D.C.: July 8, 2009).

Recovering Servicemembers: DOD and VA Have Made Progress to Jointly Develop Required Policies but Additional Challenges Remain. GAO-09-540T (Washington, D.C.: April 29, 2009).

Military Disability System: Increased Supports for Servicemembers and Better Pilot Planning Could Improve the Disability Evaluation Process. GAO-08-1137 (Washington, D.C.: September 24, 2008).

DOD and VA: Preliminary Observations on Efforts to Improve Care Management and Disability Evaluations for Servicemembers. GAO-08-514T (Washington, D.C.: February 27, 2008).

DOD and VA: Preliminary Observations on Efforts to Improve Health Care and Disability Evaluations for Returning Servicemembers. GAO-07-1256T (Washington, D.C.: September 26, 2007).

Military Disability System: Improved Oversight Needed to Ensure Consistent and Timely Outcomes for Reserve and Active Duty Service Members. GAO-06-362 (Washington, D.C.: March 31, 2006).

GAO's Mission	The Government Accountability Office, the audit, evaluation, and investigative arm of Congress, exists to support Congress in meeting its constitutional responsibilities and to help improve the performance and accountability of the federal government for the American people. GAO examines the use of public funds; evaluates federal programs and policies; and provides analyses, recommendations, and other assistance to help Congress make informed oversight, policy, and funding decisions. GAO's commitment to good government is reflected in its core values of accountability, integrity, and reliability.
Obtaining Copies of GAO Reports and Testimony	The fastest and easiest way to obtain copies of GAO documents at no cost is through GAO's website (www.gao.gov). Each weekday afternoon, GAO posts on its website newly released reports, testimony, and correspondence. To have GAO e-mail you a list of newly posted products, go to www.gao.gov and select "E-mail Updates."
Order by Phone	The price of each GAO publication reflects GAO's actual cost of production and distribution and depends on the number of pages in the publication and whether the publication is printed in color or black and white. Pricing and ordering information is posted on GAO's website, http://www.gao.gov/ordering.htm. Place orders by calling (202) 512-6000, toll free (866) 801-7077, or TDD (202) 512-2537. Orders may be paid for using American Express, Discover Card, MasterCard, Visa, check, or money order. Call for additional information.
Connect with GAO	Connect with GAO on Facebook, Flickr, Twitter, and YouTube. Subscribe to our RSS Feeds or E-mail Updates. Listen to our Podcasts. Visit GAO on the web at www.gao.gov.
To Report Fraud, Waste, and Abuse in Federal Programs	Contact: Website: www.gao.gov/fraudnet/fraudnet.htm E-mail: fraudnet@gao.gov Automated answering system: (800) 424-5454 or (202) 512-7470
Congressional Relations	Katherine Siggerud, Managing Director, siggerudk@gao.gov, (202) 512-4400, U.S. Government Accountability Office, 441 G Street NW, Room 7125, Washington, DC 20548
Public Affairs	Chuck Young, Managing Director, youngc1@gao.gov, (202) 512-4800 U.S. Government Accountability Office, 441 G Street NW, Room 7149 Washington, DC 20548

Please Print on Recycled Paper.